LIVING WHILE HUMAN

ARWINDER KAUR

Living While Human

Front cover painting of Native Mask "Re-Emergence" provided by Paul Ygartua.

Tellwell Talent
www.tellwell.ca

ISBN
978-0-2288-5134-9 (Hardcover)
978-0-2288-5132-5 (Paperback)
978-0-2288-5133-2 (eBook)

DISCLAIMER

The author of this book does not dispense advice of any kind related to health (emotional, psychological, physical, mental, or spiritual), lifestyle, diet, medications, relationships, or general well-being. Should you require assistance or advice of any kind, it is best to consult directly with your physician or health providers. The author does not claim to be an expert in any field. The contents are not offered as research in the areas of science.

If you use any information in this book for yourself, which is your constitutional right, the author and publisher assume no responsibility for your actions.

The contents of this book are based solely on the author's personal philosophy, experiences, principles, values, beliefs, and ideas. The contents are an autobiography and represent memories of events, people, and conversations as she recalls them. They do not represent the views of any other person, living or not.

TABLE OF CONTENTS

Foreword vii
Introduction xi

PART ONE: BECOMING ME

Destiny 1
Getting to Know Dadi Ji 22
Life in the New Old World 35
The Great Escape 75
Home Sweet Home 78
Acknowledging My Mentors 84
Discovering My Calling and the Compass 111

PART TWO: SIGNS OF HUMANITY IN DISTRESS

In Search of a Lost Humanity-Cultural Mutation.... 126
What of the Children? 151
The Art and Science of Nature 170
The Ponzi Scheme Economy and Corporate Dictatorship 190
Dangerous Liaisons. Corporations, Politicians, and Media-A Conspiracy of Misinformation, Deceit and Greed 218

PART THREE: RE-EMERGENCE
RESITITUTION AND RECONNECTION

A Call to Action 234
The Compass 261
Parting Thoughts 308
Ode to Social Work 319

References 321

FOREWORD

By
Tala Maillot Ygartua

Twenty-five years ago, Arwinder gifted me Daniel Quinn's book, *Ishmael.* She knew that I was passionate about environmental issues, and she knew this book would change my life since it had forever changed her own path. I was grateful to her for the spiritual adventure and all the questions it raised about our role as a species on this planet. Like so many of us, Arwinder wants to contribute to changing this world for the better. The difference is that most of us manage to happily repress the outrage and despair we feel about all the suffering and destruction we cause our planet every day. Arwinder does not repress these feelings because she simply cannot. She possesses that unique character trait called empathy, and she is true to these feelings. Her empathy towards all life on this planet is simply too strong to ignore. At the same time, her loyalty, as well as her joy and passion for life, are contagious. This is precisely why I can not think of a better person to write a book about leading a more honest and deeply connected life here on Earth.

It is rare to find someone who clearly follows their beliefs and lives their life according to them. I admire Arwinder for this and for everything she has fought for over the years in the areas of social justice and environmental issues. After reading *Ishmael*, she promoted the book everywhere, hosted call-in shows about environmental issues, met with university and college professors and recommended it for reading, volunteered at numerous environmental organizations, and helped start the idea of eco-loans at local banks. All this alongside her job as a social worker for thirty years.

It is writers like Arwinder who bare their souls to us that our future generations will thank. As a mother of four little wildings, I am constantly in search of messages to pass on to my children. I often turn to the Indigenous beliefs that were always a part of my life growing up in Vancouver. I am the daughter of artist Paul Ygartua, who spent his life painting the Indigenous people, and my family and I always discussed the importance of these ancient ways that fueled so much respect for our land and its inhabitants. Today, more than ever before, we are in desperate need to foster tolerance and empathy towards every living thing on this planet.

This is why *Living While Human* is so crucial. We have always needed to hear these brave people leading the way, but never before have we actually been so ready to listen to them. I pray this new generation will hold nothing but brave souls. I hope nothing more for them than they feel, see, and act for the world around them, as Arwinder is doing.

Tala, her husband Mathieu and their children

INTRODUCTION

This book is a micro-autobiography, not a full account of my life. There is much left out. Partly to respect the privacy of others, and partly because I'm doubtful that my life would seem all that remarkable or interesting to others. I am not a poetic writer who can describe things in lengthy flowery images, nor am I a writer with literary talent. I can only write about my experiences and what is true for me. Therefore, there are gaps in places, particularly during my two-year travel to England and India. So much happened in those years that I cannot put it all into words. But what I have done is capture some of the more memorable or poignant moments that are forever etched in my memory. This is an accurate account of my experience, certainly not a book for history classes. I, for the most part, describe things from the perspective and impressions of the young teenager I was at that time.

I write from the perspective of someone raised in Western civilization since this is where I have lived most of my life. But the issues raised about the human condition and planet are relevant and applicable regardless of where people live. The destruction of the planet and the need for action is global and requires a united global response.

The Europeans colonized and conquered territories around the globe and immigrated to these areas. Historical records more recently acknowledge that Indigenous peoples around the world inhabited these areas before the European "conquest" of the lands. This violent take-over destroyed the Indigenous way of life and has devastated those communities. Gradually and much more recently, the Indigenous people are finding their voice and their identity and rightful place as First Peoples that lived sustainably on the land. At this critical stage, the self-appointed rulers have brought the planet to the brink of total collapse. It is time for them to step aside since it is clear they only know how to destroy the planet for profit.

It is time to once again let those who lived sustainably for thousands of years lead. Around the globe, many Indigenous groups continue to live without destroying and in a sustainable way. They have the knowledge, wisdom, and connection to the land and other species to show us what we have forgotten. Many in power have not wanted us to remember, but we must: for the survival of the human race, our children and their future, and for the planet to regain its strength and biodiversity. We need help from the Indigenous people and from all those who share the desire to save the planet.

We know that nature has systems in place that must be followed and replicated. The best people to help need us to listen. They have respected nature and have done everything to protect the planet, the land, the trees, the water systems, and the biodiversity. They know how. We have little time for further delays, fake news, and false promises intended to divert and delay action. Millions can turn to billions of us that are ready for drastic change. It seems that the momentum is building in the right direction. Young people and old want to have real leadership and commitment to protecting all life on the planet.

It can't be done one tree or species at a time. It needs the whole of humanity now to create this powerful sea of change. Knowing this movement is gaining power, the corporations and corrupt politicians will devise even more methods and actions to shut this movement down. We cannot allow this. We must become the leaders and force the actions that need to be taken. Vote politicians out, boycott corporations, run for office and ensure we elect more people to office who want to save the planet. Stop feeding the corporate world that is destroying all life on the planet, pouring toxic waste so no one can rely on what we have always had: clean air, water, land, food, and biodiversity. Instead, spend money on supporting people, groups, and causes that are actively trying to do the right thing before it is too late. Break free from the chains of consumerism at the cost of the planet. This is unethical and cannot continue. No product is worth dying or killing for.

Many areas are trying to fight against the big polluters and land developers. The Amazon and other such areas are being cut and burned at an alarming rate. These groups need our money, our support, and our protests and pressure against the political and corporate machinery that is literally killing us and everything on the planet. They do not deserve our votes, our money, or our support. They must be brought down in a massive way because they have all the power to make laws and policies that allow the destruction to continue while protecting the corporate wealthy few who don't care one bit how much suffering they are creating. Politicians are not going to do anything, so stop waiting for them to take action or take the lead. If they were committed to this, it would have been done.

Young people like Greta Thunberg, Malala Yousafzai, and others around the world would not have to be sacrificing their lives to save the future of all of us. Malala survived an assassination attempt on her life, fighting for the right for girls to attend school. Greta has not been attending school to lead the protest against climate change. She endures the inconvenience (and motion sickness) of lengthy ocean journeys by sailboat to avoid using fossil fuel—something no other politicians or anyone else does. People still travel by plane. Greta eats a vegan diet as she is against animal cruelty and because raising animals to eat adds to most of the deforestation, and loss of trees vital for the planet.

As Greta has emphasized enough (!), the time for talk, meetings, conferences, forums, target dates, studies or other delay tactics is over. There is no more time. We already know what is needed. The scientists know, the ecological experts know, the Indigenous people know. We see it every day: unprecedented hurricanes, tsunamis, tornadoes, floods, fires, ice caps melting, water levels rising, and massive global catastrophes. It is not a coincidence that viruses like Covid-19 are on the rise. There will be many more. All of nature's systems are reacting to the hundreds of years of massive assault, and it must bring the ecosystem back to balance. We are the primary target for viruses and diseases because that is how the laws of biology work. Increase any population so that it becomes too large to sustain, and the result is an increase of predators. If there are too many rodents in a particular geography, their predators will grow in numbers because they have more prey to live on.

If the predators outnumber their prey, there will be a reduction of food needed to maintain their increases, and they will then get rebalanced. This is nature, and it must work this way as it is the only way to sustain the whole system.

Since we humans have made ourselves, the greatest predators consuming the planet, we have now increased beyond what the earth can sustain. As a result, there are civil wars over territories and resources and mass starvation. We see these even at the time of this writing—escalation between Israel-Palestine over territory, which never seems to resolve. The decision to invade Iraq had more to do with access to oil than to root out terrorism.

The United Nations Environment Programme (UNEP) (https://www.unep.org) suggests that over the last sixty years, at least forty percent of all intrastate conflicts have a link to natural resources.

Since we have no predators other than fellow humans and viruses, microorganisms have become our primary predators, with billions of us on the planet living in close proximity, and that number is growing every day. We have also unleashed novel, new viruses we have no immunity to by going deeper into jungles where contact with disease-spreading insects or animals occurs. Our ability to travel globally, coupled with almost eight billion of us, —we saw what happened with Covid-19. It does not mean all of us will die of it, but if we did not have the means to create vaccines, it would be very deadly for millions more. All of the infectious diseases have killed more people than all the wars combined. This is the only way nature has to bring back a balance since we have ignored warnings to do it ourselves. This is not personal, just what nature does with every species on the planet. That is how it has perfectly sustained itself for billions of years.

It is now or never. We must follow the lead. Nature has made our way forward clear. We need to stop living our lives concerned with petty things and activities like manicures, pedicures, and idolizing the Kardashians, and raising children to think the same way. Too many are doing the wrong thing. People need to admit they don't know how to save the planet, and the politicians don't know or don't want to. Listen to the Indigenous people and groups who do know how and follow their lead and their way. If enough of us, billions, do this collectively, the others will have to follow since they will have no votes or money to stay in power.

Indigenous people, women, and men from all cultures dedicated to saving the planet need to work to replace all those who are passive or actively sabotaging efforts to save the planet from further destruction. This better protects them from accepting bribes from the big corporate payoffs. Many activists and Indigenous leaders are being killed trying to save the planet for all of us.

Independent watchdog Global Witness (globalwitness.org) states that 212 defenders (of land and environment) were killed in 2019.

Activists and Indigenous leaders need our help. Stop buying non-essential things for the sake of collecting them. Increasingly, many young adults are practicing minimalism, finding they are more content with less clutter and being out of the race to collect the most toys. We need to start listening. Start voting. Start taking a stand for action. Let the Indigenous people and the many dedicated groups lead us back to a way of living that nurtures us and the planet. No more destruction. The earth cannot take anymore. We need to help. When I refer to humans, I am speaking not speaking about the Indigenous people but of the one that made themselves dominant over all others and the planet-the mutant culture.

I regard myself a feminist. I speak in this book about reducing family size by having fewer or, for some, no children. This in no way means that I am anti-procreation. Rather I am anti-suffering. From a social justice perspective, no child should be born into a situation where they are uncared for, neglected, abused, or killed. From an ecological perspective, overpopulation is causing mass suffering of children, from starvation and diseases to exploitation. It is time to remove the taboo about discussing the human population and the critical need to reduce it. Humans are not exempt from nature's powerful balancing force, and when any population is a threat to the balance and sustainability of the environment and species, it will be brought back into balance. We can do this through intention and choice, hopefully preventing continued mass human suffering and the demise of the planet. Or Nature will and must do it for us. I am for the survival of all species needed for the planet to survive. Since only one species, human, is threatening it, so humans must make drastic changes immediately to correct it. This must include reducing the number of people being added to the planet every day, year after year. This is what all species have done to survive, and so must we.

Because I am a pro-survivalist rather than an anti-procreationist, the reader should see my bluntness as a reflection of the urgent crisis the planet is in, rather than judging any individual's position on having or not having children. People who don't have children should not be stigmatized or vilified, and people who chose to have them should not be glorified. The mainstream attitude differs towards each. Having children is considered a duty and virtuous, while those who cannot biologically are considered "less" or pitied. Rarely has it been talked about that women actually choose not to have children, and if they are mentioned, they are labelled as "selfish." In the royal family, there must be an heir. A woman has no choice in the matter. It is her duty. Some men will even sire a baby with another woman to ensure an heir. At this period in time, having a child is no longer a biological choice but also a moral one.

DESTINY

Departure India/Arrival in Canada

I must have inherited my curiosity and sense of adventure about the world from my parents.

Mom often repeated the story of how she and Dadi ji came to be married. The odds were small their paths would ever cross, as their backgrounds were worlds apart. Mom was born and raised in a city, Kalka, and had a formal education. She was musically talented playing the sitar and harmonium and was a singer and a skilled dancer. She was a natural beauty and managed to look glamorous wearing simple clothes and no makeup. She had dreams of becoming a movie star in "Bollywood," Bombay, now referred to as Mumbai. She was creative: she knew how to sew, knit, and crotchet and often made her own clothes.

Dadi ji, on the other hand, was born in a small village, Rattangard of Punjab. He received religious education, and his destiny would be to become a great religious, spiritual leader. Ironically, my mother's only musical outlet was to sing religious hymns, and it was on this basis that it was decided they would make an acceptable match for marriage. It was an arranged marriage, and for many, this is still the custom today. Parents and extended family members make these decisions. As is often the case, my parents' version of events differed. She said it was a "forced" marriage; Dadi ji said it was to "save" her from being married to her father's boss. The boss was much older, not a kind or good person, and may have had an alcohol problem. But it would have been difficult for my mother to say "no" unless she was to be married to someone else. My parents were both accurate. It was definitely a better decision to prevent the marriage to the boss, so she was "saved." But from Mom's perspective, any marriage at that time was "forced" because she was not in agreement with any marriage at all.

Mom was only about eighteen years old when she and Dadi ji were married. Dadi ji was fifteen years her senior. She was naïve. In fact, no one ever had "the talk" with her, and she had no idea how children came into the world. At age nineteen, Mom was expecting her first child and asked the midwife to wake her up before the baby was born because she did not want to "sleep through it!" This was the eldest son born in Kalka in 1949.

Mom and dad at time of marriage.

Branching out

In India, one's destiny was largely preordained at birth. One rarely saw women working outside the home to earn an income. Earning an income was reserved for the men in society. Even tasks considered female (within the home) were done by men outside the home. Cooking, sewing clothes, selling goods, weaving, and carving, were done by men. Division of labour was by gender. Males were dominant and visible in the outside world, and they, along with menial (lower caste) women, would be seen doing work outside the home. Males generally followed in their father's footsteps. The career of the father would likely be carried on by the son. Women were expected to marry and take on the household responsibilities of caring for children and elders, so attending school to get a formal education was considered unnecessary.

Life was extremely difficult and living in harsh conditions was the norm. My mother would give birth to four more children in India (though one little boy passed away at six months of age). The oldest sister was born in Kanpur in 1952, Paul also in Kanpur in 1956. I was the last, born in Delhi in 1957. The family moved frequently since Dadi ji was transferred to various Sikh temples throughout the country whenever and wherever his services were required. Dadi ji performed religious ceremonies and was also a talented singer and musician, playing the harmonium and the dolik, a two-sided drum. The chance to break out of one's pre-ordained destiny was almost impossible unless someone had the financial and social support to do so. So, in the latter part of the 1950s, when the opportunity arose for the family to move to Canada, my mother convinced Dadi ji that this could not be passed up. Such was the case for us.

Our father being educated in religious studies and a respected leader within the Sikh faith, his name came up as a recommendation to fill the vacant granthi (priest) position at the Sikh temple in Queensborough (New Westminster, BC) in 1959. He was understandably reluctant because it would require him to move out to a foreign country, living alone for at least two years under a contract. If it was mutually agreeable, he could gain a permanent position, and his family could be sponsored to join him. He had heard things about life in Canada, and it was not all that positive. That it was lonely, it would be cold. People had lost their traditions; everyone worked and lived separately. He did not speak English. It was all a huge unknown, but for the sake of the children and our future, the sacrifice would have to be made. Sikhs are known to be pioneers, industrious and fearless. This would get tested now. So, in 1959, my father set out alone to a new world.

Dadiji far left and friend who recommended him Giani Sujan Singh far right.

Upon arriving, it was not long before he, in fact, began to see that the stories he had heard were true. It was cold, dark, and isolated. He was very lonely. Hardly anyone came to the temple. People had lost their traditions. Most could no longer speak Punjabi, at least not very well. Most people did not maintain the required Sikh symbols, the five "Ks": Kesh (hair), Kangha (a wooden comb), Kara (an iron bracelet), Kachera (cotton underpants), and Kirpan (an iron dagger).

He was horrified to see this. No one came to any services daily and on weekends, only a few people. Soon they would all be gone until the next weekend. It was like a ghost town. No hustle and bustle of the streets. No music playing on loudspeakers. No steady stream of people coming in to pay their respects or donate money or goods which the priest and family relied on. He was counting the minutes and had decided, once his two-year commitment was to end, he would not remain and would give notice of this. So shortly before that time, my father did just that. He submitted his letter to the board or committee. He gave them all the reasons listed above and included that he would never be able to earn enough money to pay for his family to join him or support them once they did. This was all true.

However, within the two years, positive change had started to happen within the Sikh community. His presence had begun to increase attendance slowly, and some people could see he was a learned man, a leader. They recognized they needed someone exactly like him to do what he could see was needed within the community. People began to state this in conversations and feedback. They told my father that rather than quit now, it was important to stay the course and build upon the foundation that he had just started to lay. The community wanted and needed the connection to their past, their traditions, and their deep faith. These were always important to the very life and identity of the Sikh people. In fact, people were suffering because they had lost these fundamental needs in their lives. People were lost; many struggled with alcohol abuse and domestic violence. The children had no one to help show them the traditions since their parents did not know them. Well, Dadi ji could certainly agree with this. They offered Dadi ji increased money (but it would be padded to immigration since even that would barely suffice). But more importantly, they would get funds raised, through the community, to pay for the family to travel to join him.

I guess this (and for certain, Mom's persistence) was satisfactory to "seal the deal," and that is how we came to live with our dadi ji in Queensborough in 1962.

Arwinder and family after arrival in Canada and of Arwinder about age 6.

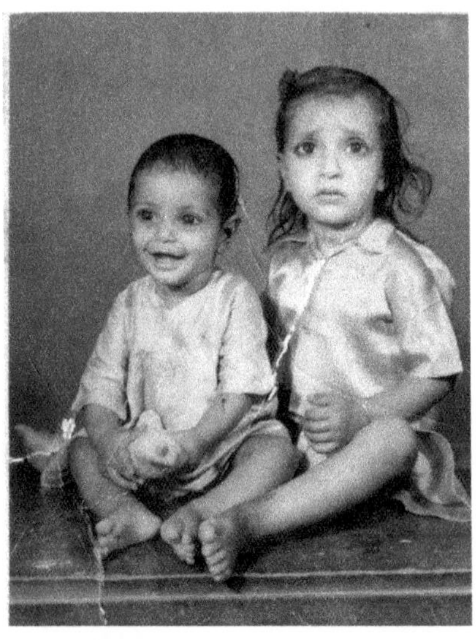

Arwinder and brother Paul India.

We became landed immigrants upon arrival, and all of us became Canadian citizens a few years later. Once we arrived (not that I recall the actual trip or arrival), we moved into the gurdwara (Sikh temple). I believe the cooking area was on the ground level with wood-burning stoves. The bathrooms were outdoors. The living area was on the second floor. The temple where the ceremonies and the actual reading of the Guru Garanth Sahib, (Sikh holy scriptures) were held was separate but beside our living quarters. Our daily routine would be to wake up and find our father sitting at the altar reading the holy scriptures where we would pay our respects, kneeling in front of the altar and bowing our heads to touch the floor. We would sit and listen for a brief time (though I may have nodded off to sleep) before getting ready to go to school. It was close, and we all walked to it each day.

Dadi ji at alter in Sikh Temple in Queensborough.

I recall the excitement when Dadi ji brought home the first car soon after arriving in Canada. It was a huge solid tank, as they all were at the time. It was evening and dark, but we insisted on going for a ride. So, we piled in. I was in the back seat. We drove for a few seconds and reached an intersection. My dadi ji turned the car left, but he cut it way too tight, and we went straight into the wide ditch. Fortunately, people were on the street talking and called for a tow truck after helping us out of the semi-submerged car. I remember being concerned that I lost a slipper in the ditch and Dadi ji telling me to forget about that. Queensborough had these ditches throughout the municipality. People with experience driving knew to make wider turns to avoid this. My father continued to make these tight turns for the time that he drove. I would roll down the window and tell the pedestrians to move away from the sidewalk, as he could drive over the curb. I only learned decades later that Dadi ji obtained his driver's license without passing a written or driver's test. We were all lucky to have survived.

Dadi ji also loved hippies because they had long hair (like Sikhs). He would pick up all that were hitchhiking and load the car up to give them a ride.

Dadi ji holding me in front of car.

During this period, there were no ESL classes, childcare workers, or cultural liaison workers, so students who could not speak English, as was the case for the two oldest siblings, were put back three grades. I was fortunate since I began in kindergarten. It was very multicultural in Queensborough (an area of New Westminster), even though most did not have a shared language. People were from Italy, Russia, India, and China. But everyone was friendly and generally happy to be in their new country. We made lifelong friends. One was of Russian descent, Powell (Paul) Janulus. He was brilliant and had a talent for learning languages. He lived with our family to learn Punjabi, Hindi, and Sanskrit. He even converted to the Sikh faith for some time. I believe he made it into the Guinness world record for spoken fluency in forty-two languages. Through him, we would later meet the Ygartua family. Paul and Joanne Ygartua were at the same party at the Janulus home in New Westminster. We watched in amazement as Paul Janulus worked the room, speaking to everyone in their native language while interpreting since many did not speak any English. There was no problem with that, and everyone enjoyed the cultural exchange and music and dance that usually followed. We still keep in touch.

Arwinder with Paul Janulus on left and Paul Ygartua on right.

Soon the temple became the community focal point it was always meant to be. Having our family actually living in the temple was also the norm in India. It became a more structured place that offered services and programs, and of course, as in every Sikh temple, langar (or community kitchen) was provided. Volunteers would arrange a particular ceremony, such as a wedding or a birth, where the Sikh scripture played an important role in choosing the infant's name. The priest would randomly open the scriptures, and the first letter of the first word would be used to name the baby. My father was happy that ultimately, it had paid off not to give up and return to India. He was now reunited with his family, making a positive contribution to the community where he was very much respected and considered to be an important leader—a mentor for the younger generation. Punjabi classes were also a regular part of the programs.

Fortunately for the community, our family was unique in that we provided services that others would usually be brought in for. Religious hymns (kirtan) were often performed by a group, like a band, if you will. They could be a variety of ensembles but usually had the base of singer(s), tabla player (hand drums), harmonium (an organ or keyboard) and other instruments depending on each individual performer. Our family was able to play numerous instruments and perform hymns for any services required, at the temple or in people's homes. Both my parents and the oldest daughter sang and played instruments. The oldest son played mainly tablas. This made it very convenient logistically and probably less costly since our family was able to provide all the necessities of religious service. We became quite the novelty and uniquely able to provide music, first strictly religious, and then later for entertainment as well—a travelling priest and band all in one.

Arwinder, parents, oldest brother and sister performing.

By chance, local filmmaker George Robertson and his partner had decided to make a documentary-style film about the challenges faced by new immigrants. Our family was selected, and in 1964 *Running to India* was produced and shown on TV for CBC. It also went on to win an award at the Montreal Film Festival during Expo in 1965. This film is now part of the vast materials about our family donated to the New Westminster Museum and Archives.

George Robertson and partner filmmakers.

This continued to be a very difficult time. The younger of the two brothers tested positive for tuberculosis (TB) shortly after our arrival in Canada. He was hospitalized at Sunny Hill Health Centre for well over a year. At that time, parents were not allowed to stay with their child in the hospital, and the visiting hours were very limited and strict. I recall I was not allowed indoors, and once a week; we would visit. If the weather permitted, he would come outside for a visit. He was very traumatized at the initial separation from the family and again every week when he was not allowed to leave with us to come home. Society did not know as much about PTSD for children with severed attachments and the lifelong negative consequences. He was no exception. He distrusted doctors for the rest of his life and eventually developed many health and medical illnesses that were never treated. Now parents can remain with their children around the clock, but perhaps because TB was so contagious, that was not possible. Attitudes now are to allow as much time as possible. It was very unfortunate, but that was the way it was then.

Coming to Canada was a double-edged sword. On the one hand, our mother embraced the new culture, as she could see that there were far more freedoms than she had before. Her children would as well. But on the other hand, the community could be very harsh and unforgiving for stepping outside the bounds expected of the wife and children of a Sikh priest. Our mom was always impeccably dressed and wore saris and makeup. That was criticized. Everything she did was scrutinized and judged. This eventually caused stress in the marriage, as Mom wanted her husband to support and defend her choices, but the community would press Dadi ji to impose more strict expectations and conformity.

Mom eventually got a thick skin and would just go about her life without giving in to the outside pressures. After all, this is what she anticipated her life would be once arriving in Canada. She did not want to be oppressed and controlled anymore by outside parties.

Soon we would move out of the Sikh temple in 1965 or so and into our purchased family home in New Westminster. I would attend Lord Tweedsmuir Elementary School, and the older two siblings went to Vincent Massy Pearson (NWSS) for high school. This area was not multicultural like Queensborough. There may have been one other student in the whole school of South Asian descent. It was not easy to fit in or make friends for myself or Paul. He was the only one wearing a turban, and that made it more difficult. I was called "Paki" or "Hindu" a few times and was more irritated that they did not even have my ethnicity correct since I was neither. Sometimes I would get hit or kicked for no reason, but I don't think I even mentioned it when I got home. The first birthday party I did get invited to and attended was at the home of a very nice family, but I was bit by a Great Dane (much larger than me). After this, it made my walk to school much longer, as I would detour if I saw a dog on any street. Fortunately, many decades later, I did get over my fear of dogs and have been blessed to have many companions.

Mom and Arwinder in front of the purchased family home.

Being the youngest in the family meant I was the default person when an item was needed from the store at that moment. The house in New Westminster was about four blocks to the store and four blocks back. One family member would send me to the store to get milk. I would get it and come back only to have a different person tell me we needed bread. I would get that, and someone else would tell me to go get another item. Each time my protests would become more emphasized, and I would complain that it would be best if people could make a list as items ran out. It was a good idea, but it was never followed, nor did it ever get me out of walking to the store in a seemingly endless loop. This, coupled with walking to elementary school every day, which was steep hills all the way there (sometimes twice if we can home for lunch), had the benefit of making me get lots of exercise.

I was not involved in extracurricular activities. Our main form of exercise was either dancing in a performance, or we kids would put on the vinyl albums, all our favourite soul and R&B music at home and literally dance for up to eight hours a day on the weekends. None of them were slow, and others were outright super fast. Music was always a passion since the start, and everyone had some form of musical talent. Dadi ji would tell people that children in the family were allowed to be born without being musically inclined.

As our life in Canada went on, I recall our father quite upset that the children had forgotten our native Punjabi language. He would give me and my brother Paul Punjabi lessons daily after school. My brother hated it, but I rather embraced it. I learned enough to read and write it on a basic level. It was as if my father had a premonition because decades later, it was my only method of communication when my father remained in India. He kept all my letters and had a good laugh at my spelling and grammatical errors but would always add how he appreciated receiving them and maintaining the connection. I was the only one who chose to do so and was extremely grateful he had the foresight to teach me my native language. Always take opportunities to learn. It is never a waste.

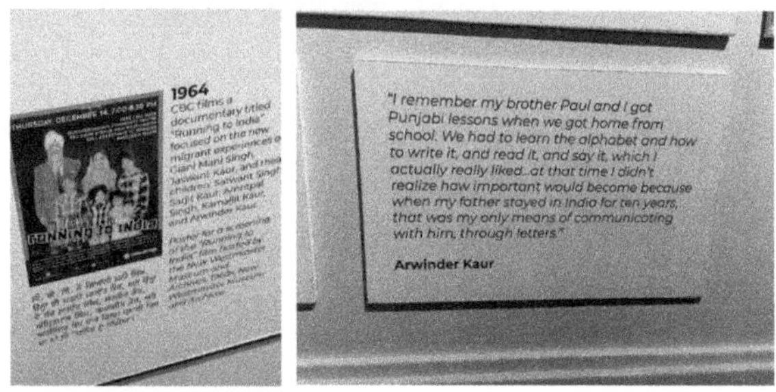

Plaques displayed at New Westminster Museum and Archives exhibition showcasing my family as part of history of south Asian community. Note the image incorrectly included Kanwaljit Kaur (Nina) but she was not born at time picture was taken.

For the first time in our dadi ji's, life he had to get employment beyond his religious duties. Dadi ji started working in the Brownley Industry Mill near the Patullo Bridge in Surrey. It was hard labour and dangerous since safety standards were not as stringent at that time. Many men had serious injuries, some even fatal. A few years into the work, in fact, Dadi ji suffered what could have been a fatal injury. The floor he was standing on gave way, and he fell about forty feet into an empty truck. Many logs fell on top of him. He was wearing a hard hat on top of his turban, but the hard hat fell off easily. Had it not been for the extra protection provided by the turban, he would likely not have survived or, at the very least, would have had a serious brain injury. The foreman later joked that the turban would need to become part of the required work clothing. Dadi ji was seriously injured, though and had a couple of back surgeries. He received a small disability pension which gradually increased every year. Dadi ji always looked at the positive side and thought a pension was fantastic. It also allowed him to begin the first of many books he authored and received world recognition for. This would eventually lead him to a life he never imagined.

In July 1967, the youngest child was born in New Westminster. She was the only one not born in India. Mom recalled how shocked the nurses were at seeing a baby with so much thick black hair. They thought she was the most beautiful baby ever, and some nurses joked maybe they should marry a South Asian man to have such a cute baby. Conversely, Mom thought there was something wrong with the other babies because they had "no hair."

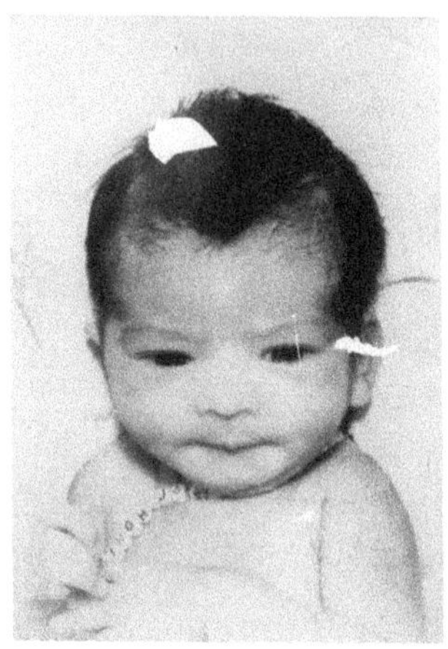

Nina as newborn.

Famous wealthy personality Korla Pandit and his wife (hollywood) with mom and Dadi ji. They had two sons and wanted to legally adopt Nina to have a daughter. The answer was "no".

Mom, too, had to get work outside the home for the first time in her life. I don't recall if it was her first job, but I recall her working as an aid or housekeeper at Hollywood Hospital. This was the real name. She used to tell us stories of how some patients seemed fine when she left work, and the next day, she was told they had died. She was very suspicious, and we did not know what to think. Decades later, I was informed by staff and the New Westminster Museum and Archives when I was giving an oral history of our family, that in fact, the hospital had been shut down due to some concerns. So, our mom must have been right with her suspicions after all. The article in the link below gives details of the type of treatment carried out there.

https://montecristomagazine.com/community/new-westminster-controversial-hollywood-hospital

In time, things would change drastically for the whole family.

GETTING TO KNOW DADI JI

Departure Canada/ arrival London England

All was not happy with my parents, which led to a separation when I was about thirteen years old. There was a multitude of stressors: financial, marital, and raising five children of varying ages in a culture that promoted individuality and freedom. Dadi ji was satisfied with a more simple, modest life. Mom felt she had been constrained with too many responsibilities and never had a moment on her own her whole life. It would become more evident that she also struggled with episodes of serious depression, and this would exacerbate all of it. I don't recall the exact moment or year, but Mom decided to move out with the daughters. The boys remained with Dadi ji at the family home in New Westminster.

At that time, in the late '60s, even in Canada, it was almost unheard of for a Sikh family to break up, and the fact that our dadi ji was a priest made it intolerable, as the community was not very understanding or accepting of this. Dadi ji and his family were expected to be "pillars" in the religious community and be perfect role models. Dadi ji had abruptly left for England after the separation, though he had no concrete plans or knew anyone there. He only knew he had to get away for a fresh start.

A couple of years later, Mom learned that Dadi ji was no longer living in the family home, and we moved back in, although the oldest brother by then was not around much since he had joined a relatively popular band of that time. The Poppy Family is a multicultural band featuring Indian instruments like the sitar, my oldest brother playing Western drums, tablas, percussion, and various instruments. They had a number of solo hits and had a real following and went on tours.

Poppy Family and our family as they leave for first international tour

One day, I overheard my mom speaking on the phone to Dadi ji in England, saying "I need to have some time to myself without the children." They came to a mutual agreement in what seemed like nanoseconds, and my three siblings and I were sitting on a plane on our way to Heathrow airport. Nina was about five or six, I was ten years older, my brother Paul was about sixteen or seventeen, and our older sister was about twenty-one or twenty-two. We had no idea how long we would be gone for. In Canada, our dad was more of the rule-setter, and we did not really spend much time having long talks or heart-to-heart conversations. I knew when he was happy or not happy about something, but he would speak to Mom about things, not directly with the children. That all changed in England.

Dadi ji later shared with us that after the family fractured, he was lost and fell into depression and total despair. He went to England and sat in the terminal staring vacantly. Fortunately, as it is with our culture, seeing an older man by himself, a family approached him and asked him if he was waiting for someone to get him? Was he staying somewhere? Did he have contacts they could call for him? Why was he there? Dadi ji could not answer any questions with anything other than "no" or "I don't know." The family took him home. Soon he began to come out of the dark place he had been in. Being with his community again with people showing him compassion, respect, and love, he became his usual fun, charming, loving, grateful self. He had a new life and became a granthi once again, and life was full of people and activity. He also shared how shattered he was being separated from the children, especially the youngest. Every time he would hear a child cry, it would open the wound in his heart, and he cried himself to sleep many nights. But now his family was coming to him.

Factory Work and Drama

One day we were in Canada going about our daily lives, the next, we moved in with Dadi ji at the Sikh temple in Eastham, England. It was a former parish in a residential area made up of rows of attached houses. Streets were much longer than a block back home in Canada. These streets seemed to wind endlessly, and it was difficult to differentiate one street or home from another. To us, it seemed the standard of living in Canada was much higher than in England. We were surprised that in many homes, people actually had a pay phone like the kind in a phone booth. They would drop coins in the longer they talked on it. The same was true for people who had landlines. They would get a bill every month as any call over like two minutes was charged, just like long-distance calls were in Canada. The same was true for hot water. In some homes, money had to be put in a machine to get hot water. Bags to carry groceries home were also extra. Once, we had to stuff all our pockets and stack the groceries to carry them home. On a rare occasion when the sun came out, we'd walk outside barefoot, and the local people thought that was odd behaviour. Since there was no hot water or bathing room at the temple, another routine became going to a public bath house. Each of us would get a room with a bathtub in it, and we would shout to the female attendant if we needed something or more hot water, etc. The toilet paper or paper towels in public washrooms either had to be paid for or were more like wax paper, which was of little practical use, but that was what was available.

Nina was enrolled in school—kindergarten, or grade one. She soon began to speak with a strong British accent.

Dadi ji spoke Punjabi, and the rest of us spoke, with what the British people referred to, as a "Canadian accent." Everyone always considers others as having an accent. Now, with Dadi ji, our lives became very structured, and there was a definite plan to travel to India as soon as we had enough money to buy airline tickets.

The textile industry in London was huge, and factory jobs were easy to get. No questions were ever asked. Despite being underage and visitors to the country, the three of us began working in a sewing factory. There were so many such jobs. One could quit a factory and walk across the street and be hired on the spot in another. Pretty much everyone working in the factories was of South Asian descent, the majority of them women. Most spoke no English, which was a blessing because we were forced to speak in Punjabi, which we rarely spoke. This daily practice for at least eight hours a day allowed us to build up our Punjabi skills to a level that we could carry on some functional conversations. The elder women in these factories were curious about us and our lives and would often ask us questions we had no answers for. The most frequent was "What is your caste?" We had never been raised as having one. In fact, this is not part of the Sikh but rather the Hindu belief system. Nevertheless, many people still formally or informally observed this aspect in their lives.

When we asked our dadi ji about this, he would explain it was not part of our life or Sikh faith, but to be a bit provocative (Dadi ji liked to challenge these belief systems and/or superstitions), he would tell us to answer that we were near the lowest caste. Of course, no one would want to admit to this if it were true. So, we told the elders what Dadi ji suggested, and they would converse among themselves and decide that could not be true. Since we had made it to Canada, had the means to travel, we must have been mistaken and were from a higher caste. This pattern was repeated many times with many people, and it became a family "inside joke."

Every morning the three of us walked to the subway station to take the train to Whitechapel. Our dadi ji made us tea, chai, and breakfast, and we packed our lunches the previous night. Every day we would see the same people dressed up on their way to work, and it was usually so busy that often we stood in the train packed like sardines. Sometimes the train would make abrupt turns, causing people to drop things or collide with each other.

Every day, for at least eight hours, we worked and took our predetermined coffee and lunch breaks. Bundles of clothes would be brought to each station, and I would cut excess threads and put them back into a bundle. My older sister was able to use a sewing machine, so she was placed in that station. My brother Paul used a press with a foot pedal to iron clothes. Some would get paid by the piece and others by the hour. At the end of each week, we would get a small envelope with our cash inside. To us, it did not seem like much by the time we paid for the weekly train pass, and we handed the rest to our dadi ji to save towards the airfare to India. For us, there was no cost to living in the Sikh temple since room and board were provided. People often made donations of food, clothes, or cash. My older sister and I shared a bedroom on the lower floor of the temple. This is where the main hall and eating area were for langar.

Sometimes on the weekends, when we first woke up, we would forget we were living in a temple, open the door yawning and in pyjamas, only to shut the door immediately, seeing the place filled with beautifully dressed people attending a wedding. We had no notice of what events would be happening, or we were just not told. We would have to wait for the crowd to dissipate, find an opportune time and run upstairs to the washroom to brush our teeth and wash our face.

Dadi ji was a wonderful, attentive parent. He had dinner ready for us when we came home from work every night. His food tasted excellent, and this was really the first time he did the cooking in the home. Nina and Dadi ji were inseparable and Dadi ji loved being a role model, telling her stories and making up some magical answers if he did not have a scientific one. She became very curious and inquisitive, and her "whys" became never-ending. Dadi ji had a clever and witty sense of humour and would often do and say things just to get a laugh. He was extremely diplomatic and stayed out of politics. He was also a very disciplined person and maintained a very strict schedule. He would wake up early, drink his chai, and do his writing, sometimes up to twelve hours a day. Midday, he would go out for a very long walk up to about two hours minimum at a very brisk pace.

If we went somewhere with him, he refused to take transportation. We would constantly whine, telling him to slow down as we could not keep up with him. He would also trick us into walking miles at a time by telling us we were "almost there." We were "almost there" for about three-four hours. We would threaten to stop walking, and we did. He would point to a building and say, "It is right there." That seemed close enough, but once we got to that building, it was the next landmark. He managed to get us to the destination, but he had a real mutiny on his hands. His tactics worked, and we got in better condition whether we wanted to or not.

London, being a fashion hub, people, especially women, dressed in the exact same outfit the very same day they arrived in the shops. People wore huge platform shoes and flare pants.

We were surprised to see ATMs as this was around 1972-73, and we had never seen these in Canada. Pubs were everywhere, and a woman my sister and I took classical Indian dance lessons from took us to one before we left for India. I was only about fifteen or sixteen, but no one asked for ID. Of course, we had no alcohol, but the sandwiches were very tasty. The atmosphere in the pub was very relaxed.

After our first classical dance lessons, our legs were weak and wobbly walking down the stairs. Our muscles were protesting since the style of dance involves holding uncomfortable poses for long periods of time. Our instructor had the thighs to show for it. The lessons were one night of the week, and we came home and after dark. We would talk ourselves into a frightful state and panic while walking the long winding dark streets. We would remind ourselves, "This is Whitechapel, the same streets that Jack the Ripper murdered many women." This realization would cause us to start running as fast as we were able—achy, trembling muscles and all.

The only regular social event of our weekends was "marathon movie watching." Every weekend we would watch at least a doubleheader, which would be two Hindi movies at least three hours each. With the trailers and intermission, it was about an eight-hour venture. It was the first time we went to Southall, referred to as "Little India." We had never seen so many places to shop and eat and buy *samosas* at a movie theatre.

Racial Tensions

Tensions were high in the city. We noticed much more racial hostility. Not absent, but this was not as palpable and overt in Canada. South Asians in England were in a particularly bad situation at this time. The "aristocratic" South Asians had been ejected from Kenya, Nairobi in Uganda by Idi Amin.

Many of the African people in England were not friendly to us, assuming we were part of "that" community. And many Caucasians (white people) did not like any of us in the country. There were two incidents that really stand out. One happened when a child taunted my sister and me with racial slurs as we were walking down a street. We followed the child to his home in hopes of speaking with the parents about this. We were met by a very inebriated, belligerent father. He proceeded to push us out of the walkway while hurling further racial verbal abuse at us. We were very upset but quickly understood where the child had learned it from.

Another incident occurred at one of our favourite restaurants. It was truly the best curry we ever had, and believe me, we were experts. We sat waiting for our order, and in fact, there were no other patrons in the restaurant. The owner was a petite stature, friendly South Asian man standing nearby. Suddenly the door flung open, and a Caucasian man entered. He was very drunk and yelled some racist remarks. He approached the bar area where lots of wine and cocktail glasses had been stacked on the counter. With one huge sweep, he flung them down on the floor, smashing them into pieces. We sat frozen at our table, probably with our mouths open in shock, looking terrified. We wondered, *what could this nice little man do against this tall, angry drunk man?* We had no idea; we were worried.

The owner disappeared into the kitchen. For a moment, we thought the drunk man might turn his attention to us since no one else was present. But the kitchen door swung open, and the owner came back holding a small container in his hand. He pulled out his hand, shaped it into a fist, and tossed red powder towards the drunk man. With absolute precision, the powdery substance dissipated into the air and into the drunk man's eyes. He began to scream in agony. He stumbled out of the restaurant, and we barely began to sigh in relief when he stumbled back in. He went straight into the washroom. He washed his beet-red eyes as best as he could and stumbled out again. This time, for good. The owner apologized to us for the terrible incident and just went on as before, as though this was a regular occurrence, which it probably was.

He cleaned up the mess of broken glass. Police were not called. Nothing was reported. He showed no anger, remained completely calm. We felt very humbled and left with tremendous respect at how the owner handled the whole situation. We continued to go to his restaurant, never having any concerns for our safety again. We later learned pepper is the main ingredient used in mace. We saw this day that regular chilli or cayenne powder was more dangerous when not ingested.

Sikh Community Support

The local community had established a strong relationship with our dadi ji, and there was always an outpouring of support whenever a need arose. The need would arise more than once. This became necessary when airline tickets purchased to go to India had to be repurchased since the airline company had gone bankrupt. As soon as a plea by community members went out, donations were made, and we were able to get our tickets to leave for India. It was heartwarming to see how much the community began to grieve once the date for leaving was set. It seemed like every family in the area wanted us to come to their house for lunch or dinner before we left. The schedule for these goodbyes became so tight, we were double-booked every single day, leaving us just enough time to literally "eat and run" to the next house. This went on for weeks. It was great to spend so much time with Dadi ji. He was hilarious and would do and say things to make us laugh. He was saying grace like an auctioneer because we were so pressed for time between meals. We would all give each other the subtle smile to let him know we got his joke. I saw him in a very different way in this new world he had come to and created in England.

The experiences with the Sikh community were more familiar to what Dadi ji was accustomed to and wanted. Dadi ji seemed at a very happy, peaceful place. In England, the Sikh community was more populated, and their established ties to the Sikh faith and culture were deep. Dadi ji was also respected due to the many books he had authored. His first was a book of axioms called *Anmol Bhol.* It is the only one translated into English, made available in England during our time there.

Living in England for such a long period of time and being in the workforce with so many south Asian women taught me much about life and hard work. They seemed to really like the fact that, as women, they were earning a living, and I could see the sense of comradery they had: a family outside the home. The women would share their lives, how things were for them at home and share some laughs. Though they had to look after families when they got home from work, not really having time to them selves, the work they did outside of home was paid work and gave them a sense of accomplishment and a feeling of some independence. I could see how the money did not go very far. What little time there was left when working full time.

At least for us weekends were for relaxing. We would have time for that again soon.

So, it went this way for about thirteen months, and the day arrived for us to leave for our epic trip to India. A critical event happened that would cause us some complications during our travels. Dadi ji's contacts in

England took care of business, such as getting his visitor's visa extended during his stay in England. However, due an oversight, the four children never had theirs extended beyond the initial six-month visitor visa. As we prepared to embark on our plane to India, the customs/immigration official pointed this out. We had resided in the UK illegally for over six months. If we ever returned to the UK, there could be a problem with re-entry. Well, we brushed this off since we were on our way to India for an indefinite period of time and then hoped to return to Canada. We also had a record of vaccinations from England prior to going to India, though we never had any of the vaccines. This alone could be catastrophic for most travellers; miraculously, we turned out to be the exception to that rule. No one got any exotic or serious illness while we lived in India, almost a year. The other issue, however, would have huge implications, but for now, "ignorance was bliss."

LIFE IN THE NEW OLD WORLD

Departure England/Arrival India

New Delhi, Fear, and Culture Shock

It must have taken us three days to travel from England to India because our ever frugal and practical Dadi ji booked us on a flight that must have made twenty-eight stops, probably, in every country along the way! This included a stopover in Beirut, where we had to clear through customs before proceeding on. The airport was secured with heavily armed guards wearing militia or military-style uniforms, with rifles in hand or hanging from their side belts. It felt very dangerous, and the tension was high. This was the first time I actually saw an armed security force, and it was terrifying. We just tried to keep our head down, listen intently, follow directions accurately and avoid being shot. To us, this seemed to be a real possibility.

We paraded through in single file; my older sister and I were even searched under our clothes, thankfully, by a female and behind a curtained, private room. The Middle

East in the 1970s was not a very friendly, welcoming place to visit. I believe there was tension between the regions (the Middle East and England), and these guards expressed this in their body language and on their faces. The whole experience was quite an ordeal, and we felt relieved to be departing without any further incidence.

So, after what felt like three days, we finally landed at the New Delhi Airport, the capital of India. The capital? I thought this must be a village as everything seemed so old and decrepit. There was nothing that resembled what I considered a "modern" city. The lineups were long and barely moved for what seemed to be an eternity, and there did not appear to be much in the way of technology. I observed some gigantic insects that were crawling everywhere and almost seemed to be emerging from clothing. They may have been black carpet beetles.

Some of us were wearing real gold bracelets under our long-sleeved blouses. They were given by families in England upon our departure to India. They wanted the jewelry hand-delivered by those they trusted to relatives in India. It was the only sure way that it got to the intended party. Any other means, including the postal or other formal delivery services and the goods would simply disappear. After "clearing" customs (as I am sure we did not have all the necessary paperwork), "culture shock" hit—as it is rightly called. It happened as soon as we stepped outside the airport and onto the street. This was truly like arriving on an alien planet, and I often reflected throughout the days and months to come. How could it be possible that people living in some parts of the world could be living in such an alien and "primitive" way (in my assessment)? To me, it was like going into a time travel machine, back a few hundred years!

Travelling in India in 1973 was not for the faint of heart. Yes, I was born there but had left for Canada with my mom and siblings when I was four years old, and I had not retained a single memory of it, and now, ten to eleven years later, the adventure in India began. All senses were hit simultaneously, like a powerful tsunami. It was difficult to focus on a single sense since they were equally overwhelming.

The eyes were taking in a barrage of scenes that looked like they belonged in a movie set. There was no way this place was part of the same planet, Earth, that I knew. How could someone get on a plane, travel a few hours (or days if you are frugal), and arrive in a part of the world that looked, well, "pre-historic." Distracted from the visual landscape, I focussed on the more immediate time and place and noticed that an angry mob of men, women, and children had surrounded us and were "begging" for money. I say "begging" because what we were actually subjected to was more a mugging. The hostile and desperate-looking faces, with outstretched hands, demanding money, were clearly not going to allow us to leave without getting some. I recall trying to explain I only had change in English currency, but the reply was a chorus of "we don't care" in various languages. We all emptied our pockets as quickly as possible, and the "mob" soon turned their attention to another group of new arrivals.

I had only been on the streets of India for a few minutes and had already experienced what felt like an unarmed robbery. No time to think about that anymore, as we were now hailing a "taxi" or a car with individuals that drove it. Fighting through a crowd and barrage of voices shouting to come to their cars, while others would be more aggressive and start pulling on our suitcases, we quickly had to choose which one to take. Of course, it would be up to Dadi ji. The rest of us kids were going to be of no help deciding anything or suggesting anything. We were in Dadi ji's territory, or country as it were. Dadi ji had not experienced us being this tongue-tied ever. Not a word was uttered.

We got into a large, four-door vehicle, but three adult men sat in the front, whispering and taking long looks at us and our belongings. They did not engage in small talk, and that feeling of tension and danger resurfaced as to signal that this, too, was another potentially unsafe situation. My sister and I could hardly swallow, and we must have looked as though we already had a gun to our heads. We seriously doubted we were going to reach our destination and wondered if we would be kidnapped, robbed, raped, and killed. At this time, in India, "foreigners" were thought to be living in gold palaces with wealth beyond imagination. We knew this was not true, but with perceptions and real life, these things are subjective and relative. In Canada, we lived just above the poverty line. But compared to the average person in India, we might as well have been British aristocracy. If they robbed us of all our money, it would seem like no crime to them since we could just get more. In reality, we would have been in a very bad crisis situation as my dadi ji had no additional funds, nor did he have credit cards, and ATMs did not exist, even in Canada at that time. Every day it was like this: a feeling of having evaded certain death or some tragedy. On the streets, it very well could have been.

The youngest, Nina, was only about six and, fortunately, seemed oblivious to everything. As long as Dadi ji was holding her near, she was happy and curious. We finally exhaled upon arriving at our destination.

We were so grateful to be unharmed, though it felt as if we had dodged a bullet. This feeling became a regular feature of our lives. I did not know much about India but based on what I already witnessed in the first hour of arriving, I knew it was going to be an experience like no other. There would be some harsh things I would have to see and somehow learn to accept.

I Love Lucy in New Delhi

The family we would be staying with in New Delhi were Sikh, and the father had served as a granthi as well. Dadi ji had known them his whole life. They were a very warm, accommodating family. We would stay here for the first weeks or months. It became a hub to stay between places we would visit, often by train. The first few days were sometimes awkward as we had to learn there were different areas one would use. One was in the main part of the house, the outside veranda. It had a tiny room made of concrete and had a concrete basin filled with cold water. There was no running water or faucets. This was the area to bathe or urinate. The water would drain out from a small opening on the wall near the ground. Otherwise, one went to an outhouse. Most of India didn't have flush toilets. We had to squat to do everything, such as cooking, cleaning, bathing, and going to the latrines. That was difficult and put a lot of strain on the upper legs. Eventually, we gained the strength to manage better.

The family we stayed with was a novelty in the area because they had the only TV (black and white), and the children nearby would drop in in the late afternoon. They all sat quietly on the floor, watching in amazement the images on the screen. They were watching *I Love Lucy* and loved it, even though they could not understand English.

It was rare at this time for anyone to keep pets of any kind. This family had a German shepherd, and he would attack if he sensed the need. He was a real guard dog. He would only bark and growl at anyone that came to their home that did not wear a turban.

Me left and sisters sitting with family we stayed with in Delhi.

Experience for the Senses

We went to many tourist sites and many off-grid. Each minute outside was eventful. The heat was stifling; our clothes were drenched and clung to our bodies. The smells and sounds were unfamiliar and overpowering. Buses had people hanging off the sides, sometimes by just the tip of a finger, or piled on the rooftops. Motorcycles sped by with a family of four on the seat and a small child sitting relaxed on the handlebars. Only the father was wearing a helmet. The woman sat with both legs sideways, draped in a long, flowing, beautiful sari, sometimes holding a newborn. There were rickshaws and three-wheel scooters, tuk-tuks, and cows, goats, and vendors. We saw a person on the ground with blood all over his shirt, in obvious pain and distress, while people stood around him arguing about who was at fault for the traffic accident. I heard no sounds of a siren, nor was there any indication that an ambulance or paramedics would arrive to offer any type of assistance to someone seriously injured, and perhaps even dying, on the street.

The streets were scattered with blind people, people with no limbs, some of them on a handmade cart with wheels, just above the ground, that they might push with their hands. There was food being cooked and sold on streets by vendors, each shouting what they were selling. Some areas had open sewage; others were clean and pristine. The traffic seemed to be completely out of control with no rules as far as we could tell. The poverty was overwhelming as many people were living on the streets or on the platforms of train stations. Families with children slept there and brushed their teeth on the edge of the platforms. Men slept on their rickshaws with a light blanket. If you needed to hire one, you could approach any one of them at any time and wake the driver up. Every type of transportation of people or goods was filled beyond the width or height it could hold. Some vehicles, large trucks actually, leaned so far to one side they looked about to fall over. It was all too much to process. Unbelievable scenes were everywhere. The traffic and roads were almost incomprehensible.

People hung off the sides of moving trains as well. I saw people earning a meagre living while placing themselves at death's door every day. One example was when we were all crammed into a train, literally unable to move. Our father never believed in travelling "first-class," whatever that may have looked like. As the train was chugging along, suddenly we saw a woman climb in through the open window. She had a metal bucket filled with dry lentils, small slices of lemons, and small square sheets, cut out of newspaper. She made her way through the compartment selling as many as she could. Then with no fanfare or assistance, she climbed back out a window, hanging on to the side of the train, making her way into the window of the next compartment.

People were known to die often. I remember thinking how much money stunt actors in a Hollywood movie made. They do not do feats nearly as risky, or for long hours, every day of their lives. This woman barely earned enough to live for a day. This is not to suggest that it is good or right for people to have to survive this way, that it is just or fair. We do, however, need to be aware of the struggles people face, but that we are not alone in that, it exists within all life on the planet. The differences are that we create human suffering (not the same as struggling). Humans, alone by our actions and inactions, create the suffering inflicted upon every species on the planet and the planet itself. More on this later.

Blackouts and Stunts (Written for Writing Class)

The train slowly approached the station and screeched to a halt, slightly passing the stop point. It was crowded beyond capacity. People literally hung out the windows, some casually with just one arm or a few fingers hanging on to a ledge or window. Others, including me, stood in the toilet facility. The stench hung thick in the air. The train was fueled by coal, and a dark cloud of smoke and soot was a constant presence and, like a fine mist, covered our faces and clothes. But it was like that in most places we went to in India. I was about sixteen years old in 1973, and India was not the country it had become when I returned in 2005 at age forty-seven. I am not sure if there was a first-class category available, but Dadi ji was far too practical to waste money on anything he considered to be frivolous comforts. Dadi or "Dadi ji" (the more respectful term we learned to use) suggested "we" go eat something at a canteen during the stop. Of course, it was "we" since my older sister and I went everywhere together, including the latrines! We had always been very close, and travelling in a foreign country, where we often feared for our safety, meant we never ventured anywhere on our own. We were an inseparable team and often knew what the other was thinking without exchanging a word. The smallest glance or gesture was all that was needed for us both to understand what was being referred to.

Since we were hungry, our bodies stiff and achy, we thought it could benefit us to stretch and take a walk. My sister and I stepped onto the platform. Since things were notoriously behind schedule in India, we felt we would have ample time to eat something in leisure. The platform was teeming with masses of people, children crying and playing, homeless people gurgling as they brushed their teeth, and a mother washed up the children. The clang of pots and cups could be heard among the sounds of people shouting out whatever they were selling. "Garam chai," "taxi," "daal" (lentils), was almost deafening. Beggars demanding money was a constant, difficult to ignore.

We hesitantly approached a very crowded canteen, and out of habit and necessity, began to survey whether it was safe or not. Suddenly, the raucous conversations went silent, and all eyes turned to focus on us. To our horror, we noticed there was not a single woman in the establishment besides us, and the faces that had their eyes locked on us made us feel violated, as though they were undressing us with those eyes. Instinctively, we both started to leave, but a waiter, who was obviously very sensitive to our plight, immediately assured us that it was fine to enter, and he showed us to a table. Though we were still reluctant, there was something about the waiter that eased our fears enough that we sat down to eat, though we made sure we were close to the entrance in case we needed to leave in a hurry. We had no idea how true that would become.

Since people only made quick stops in the canteens, our food was served on a huge leaf. It was a nice vegetarian meal consisting of some spicy daal, rice, a roti, and a strong, sour, hot pickle. It was easy to be vegetarian in India during our ten-month stay because the food was so fresh and well prepared. I am sure it was also much safer to eat. We were warned to stay away from all street vendors, but we had been eating everywhere and never got sick. Against all advice, we even failed to have any vaccines or medications before travelling to India, but again, we had no ill effects. We concluded we had natural immunities from being born there because others had nightmare stories about becoming deathly ill as soon as they arrived in India.

We had to pay at the time the food was ordered, and we sat enjoying our food. Without warning, everything went dark. There was a power outage again, as this was a very frequent occurrence in India. It would happen any time and could last anywhere from minutes to hours or days. But it happening now, while we sat in a dark room filled with hungry-eyed men licking their lips, was so terrifying for us that all we could do was bolt. And that is exactly what we did, probably setting an Olympic record in the process.

As if being in a cold sweat fleeing for our lives was not enough, we noticed the train had begun to leave the station. What? How could it possibly be leaving early? The only good fortune we had was that the train was slow to build up speed. We were able to catch up to it and jump in through the open door while it was on the move. Our dadi ji looked at us in disbelief, trying to process that he had just witnessed his two meek daughters jumping onto a moving train just in the nick of time. But what happened next was truly amazing and what I regard as the true essence of India and its people. The waiter from the canteen had run right behind us, our food in hand, jumped into the train, handed us our food, and jumped back onto the platform, going back to work as though it were an ordinary, daily occurrence. And it probably was.

I reflected on why that waiter had made us feel safe, and he revealed it at that moment. He was not going to allow anything bad to happen to us, and he surely was not going to let us leave with an empty stomach. That is how things happen in India. Things just happen, and people just adapt and get through it. That power outage that sent us out from the canteen in a panic, terrified, also allowed us to leave at the exact moment we should have, or we would have missed that train, the one that never in all of history has ever left early.

*

Surveying the scene, I saw a chaotic, out-of-control, disorganized and lawless place, but no one seemed to be in any state of panic or concern. After being on the road for one day, I surmised that everyone in India must be killed in traffic accidents. How could anyone not? To an outsider, the driving conditions were not only unsafe, they were outright treacherous and nothing short of suicidal. I remember thinking, *OK, all you professional race car drivers, go ahead, try it!* But the people born and raised in India had it in their DNA. They had what was required to be a driver or a pedestrian, for that matter, without being killed. Basically, the simple rule is if you are a pedestrian or vehicle in front of someone, it was totally incumbent on the person behind you to take all necessary steps to avoid a collision or at least a serious one. Slightly hitting, tapping, or sideswiping a vehicle or person (make that any inanimate or living thing) is totally accepted, and no one stops to query if everyone is fine or to exchange personal information since no one will be filing any report. To add to the challenge, no one drives an automatic and at that time, AC was out of the question.

The constant noise added to the assault on the senses, and the congestion of people added to the feeling it was all chaotic. How could this be the country where the peace and spiritual movement came from? It seemed too much of a paradox to me, but I had much to learn with the journey just beginning. The senses take everything in, and the time for full reflection, analysis, understanding, and appreciation would come later. I would continue to learn India was made up of very resilient people who had to learn how to survive and that my values and priorities were luxuries many others did not have. My father would refer to anything that wasn't a necessity as "frivolous" or "petty," and I came to agree with this.

But having real toilets, I did not consider to be "frivolous." At that time, the early '70s, there were no flush toilets except for the very rich and privileged, and attending to toilet needs became one of my most dreaded experiences. In Kalka, the outhouse was a tiny space with no electricity. Bricks stacked up, one for each foot, and one did everything in India by squatting, and this was no exception. We had candles that provided dim light. We could see numerous creatures just inches away from us as they were all over the wall surrounding us. We were too stupid to be scared since we did not know there were scorpions, and they were very lethal. We shuddered in terror once we were told, and it really made it difficult to relax. One wanted to just get out as soon as possible. If it was not long enough time, we would just dash out and come back later. For decades I was plagued by frequent nightmares where I run from one stall to another trying to find a clean one that I could tolerate. I was grateful to wake and discover it was only a bad dream. But at that time, it was reality. We learned to time our toilet habits around the time the latrines were cleaned by the unfortunate caste of people referred to as the "untouchables."

Recycling everything in India was not a fad or designed to be politically correct, but out of sheer necessity.

The government did not provide much-needed infrastructure or services. People had to fend for themselves. We watched a child follow behind a cow to collect the cow dung. This was slapped into flat patties and stuck on the side of the wall to dry and use as fuel. There was no centralized electricity in villages, and some people obtained electricity in their homes by running wires onto the main grid. Safety was never a basis upon which to do or not do something, and if someone got hurt or killed, well, that was life. Survival was the need that drove everyone and everything. Do or die was never truer than what I experienced and witnessed in India.

There were insects never seen before. Some were just bigger than what I had seen before, like ants and rats. There were moths, centipedes, geckos, scorpions, vultures, bats, and monkeys. Sometimes, to get some water to drink at night, we switched the lights on in the kitchen, and the entire floor would be moving. We just waited until they scurried out, not knowing what they were or if they were dangerous. We never actually came across any snakes, thankfully.

I recall how Mom would reminisce about living in India. How much activity there was in the streets and markets. Everything was just out of one's door, or it would come to your door since vendors would often have a cart on wheels and work their way through the streets. Even among the houseboats in Kashmir, people in canoes paddled by selling anything you wanted, or they would get it if they did not. One just had to ask. People never pre-arranged visits, they just turned up at your door. Mom felt Canada was so lonely. Everyone sheltered up in their homes—nothing going on in the streets with no festivities outside at all times. I could certainly see what she meant. Every inch of the markets was jammed with a cart or cubby hole.

But the markets were separated by products. One street would have pots and pans, another shoes, another material for making clothes, and it went like that for what seemed like an eternity. How would anyone make any money with so much competition? The way it works is that you go to the vendor that you have some relationship or history with. So, people in that sense are not really competing because they have reliable customers that will only buy from them. The competition comes when they are selling to tourists like us. They could spot us a mile away, even though we made sure we dressed in traditional Indian wear. It must have been our body language because we could not figure out any other way. Once they recognized the "newbies" the frenzy of activity would begin. Vendors would use various strategies to get our attention: showing their products, best prices, best quality only they had, or even follow behind us negotiating a price. If we agreed, we all had to walk back to the outlet to complete the sale. And they knew how to drive a hard bargain and would only give in once you seriously walked away. The hours of operation were flexible as long as a potential sale was pending.

The street vendors offered every product and service known to man. I saw a vendor that had what appeared to be some rusty looking "dental tools" where people could come to get something attended to. Other than pulling out a tooth, I could not imagine anything else that the vendor could, or should, be doing to anyone! Some were only selling a few perfectly hand-sliced coconuts or fruits. I could not fathom anyone earning enough to live on, but people learn to be resourceful and to be street smart was part of that. My dadi ji would joke about how everything you bought in India had been so diluted that if you took poison to kill yourself, you would not die!

Dental tools.

We travelled to areas that differed drastically. Each area seemed to have its own dialect, style of dress (even if slightly), and style of cooking. Most were vegetarian, but in many areas near the coastline, people ate fresh fish. Some ate lamb or goat. No one ate beef. Vendors were all over; no one needed a license to sell anything. Many people earned enough to eat for the day.

Heavenly Food on Earth

Food was bought or delivered fresh and cooked daily. There was no need or desire for leftovers. Most people never had refrigerators. None of the people we stayed with ate meat, and the vegetarian food they prepared was heavenly. The ingredients like vegetables, herbs, rice, milk, cream, ghee, yogurt, pickles, rotis, everything was made fresh daily. Chai could be made with numerous flavours added like cardamom, fennel, ginger, cloves. Lassi, a drink made from fresh buttermilk, could be made salty or sweet, and the sweet one had fresh rose water that smelled very fragrant and like rose perfume. The cream that came from water buffalo was rich and creamy. All the dairy foods so tasty were all made in the home. I have never been able to replicate the taste, nor can anyone. Nothing bought was processed or mass-produced, and it was the most organic food one could eat. In Canada, we would have to pay a higher price for that; but of course, the people who lived there just saw it as their local food. Nothing complicated or special about it. We loved the mangos so much that we had buckets with cold water filled with mangos and ate them all day long. These were supersized mangos, juicy and sweet. After binging on them, I had the worse case of canker sores in my mouth due to their high acid content. Every part of my mouth was full of them, and I was in excruciating pain. I was unable to eat or drink anything without causing more pain. I had to wait days for them to heal before I could resume eating or drinking.

Arwinder left back row and Dadiji far right and Nina in front eating sugar canes in village.

During the lengthy time period there, we were never actually robbed, and the only thing that was taken while we slept in on our many journeys was the food, we had packed with us. We could understand that. Another time my brother had stayed behind with family in Delhi while we went to visit relatives elsewhere. Word had gotten out that "foreigners" were staying in this home. There was an assumption we would have lots of expensive items. Ironically, we were probably the only people who had no gold jewelry as is commonly worn. We had more traditional clothing made for our trip to India. Beyond that, we were not collecting high-priced items. Luckily my brother had woken up and thwarted the robbery, so everything remained intact. The only thing of value we lost were a couple of rolls of undeveloped film of the Taj Mahal and adjoining sites.

Amritsar, Temples, and Cooking

We had no stove or ovens to cook with. We learned, without much success, how to light firewood to cook our food on a metal pail that had clay around the lip formed like a claw to place the pot on. There was that or use a kerosene stove. Well, after we almost died of smoke inhalation and caused an evacuation, it was decided (probably by the community) that we get a kerosene stove. This meant, though, that unless we had multiple "stoves," things had to be cooked one at a time.

Local polishing steel dishes with sand.

With no hot running water, we would take quick baths, where we mainly soaped ourselves and our hair and dumped cold water over ourselves—speed being the main goal. Our little sister found it very distressing and would scream so loud during her baths that our dadi ji would come to see what we were doing to her that was causing her all this pain. "We are just giving her a bath," we would reply. It did not occur to us that maybe we should warm the water up for her. We thought that it was going to take too much effort to get a fire going, and we would only be able to warm a small amount at a time. We accepted that we had to rough it out. But our sister being only about six or seven did not share our approach.

In hindsight, we were very relaxed about sending her out to bring us ice cream from the local vendor. We never considered she could be a victim of abduction or harm. Thankfully, it all ended well in that regard.

Many things we thought of as of no consequence were actually taboo. Once, I showed my skills at shuffling cards and fanning them out perfectly, only to be scolded by Dadi ji. He very sternly asked who taught me to do this? This was an activity associated with men and gambling. So, we played cards under the blankets with a flashlight at night.

My older sister and I loved the beautiful saris. The colours, embroidery, and sequins in them were dazzling. We wore them to go to the market. We were quite proud of ourselves for dressing "culturally appropriate." Once again, we were off the mark and got a severe scolding for "walking around half-naked." Apparently, the dress was not appropriate for unmarried women, especially for daughters of a granthi.

Also, it was customary to refer to every male as a "brother or uncle." Sometimes my sister and I were expected to do a form of service for hours. We would be at a house, and the women were busy preparing for some occasion where a lot of food was to be prepared. No one asked us. We would be assigned some duty, like peeling and cutting onions with no determined end time. After some hours, we gathered the courage to suddenly announce we had to leave. Without waiting for permission, we made a quick exit. Our dadi ji just took it in stride.

Other customs would lead to misunderstandings or confusion. For example, in Canada, if we offered a guest something to drink and they said no, that was the end of it. In India, we did the same. Once the guest was offered tea and said no, we would go back to other tasks or just sit down for a visit. After a while, our dadi ji would ask why we were not bringing tea and snacks, and we explained they said "no." He educated us on the common ritual. The guest was expected to say "no," and we were expected to bring it anyway. It was considered impolite to seem eager to accept. The other thing people could not understand was how people from a wealthy country could be so skinny. My brother and I were particularly skinny, but not because we did not eat. We just were. The general consensus was that we needed to be fattened up. We also would honestly tell people when they offered that we did not want tea or food, but due to their customs, that was not an option, and all kinds of things would be brought.

I was most touched by the generosity of people who literally had nothing. In the village, people lived in one room. The floors were the earth with cot beds (ropes weaved in a criss-cross manner with a frame and four legs). That was the bed, no mattress. It was tightly woven and was very uncomfortable by our standards. Our bodies ached the next day. There was light from a single bulb. The family made some eggs for us, and that was considered a luxury item. The people were very humble and showed us tremendous respect and kindness.

A Life and Death Situation

One traumatic event happened when an older friend of my father's dropped in to visit him (as is the custom), but our father was not in. We offered him some tea, and he was waiting for our dadi ji to return. He told us he had just come from getting an injection of some kind, something he routinely would get without any problem. But he started feeling very unwell. As he got up to walk towards the door, he started to collapse. He stumbled back onto the bed and began struggling to breathe. We did not know what was happening, and my brother ran out trying to get help. My sister and I were in a state of panic as it was clear the person was not getting better. By the time someone, including a doctor, I believe arrived and gave him an injection, it was too late, and there was froth coming out of his mouth. He suddenly stopped and became still. The doctor announced, "He is gone." I was incredulous and surmised that perhaps this doctor was not very competent and that he must be mistaken. I kept telling him he couldn't be dead and maybe they need to call someone else for help.

We were told that he had come from getting a penicillin injection and did not wait afterwards because there was no fear about a reaction because he had it before. But on this occasion, apparently, he had an allergic reaction that proved to be fatal. We were just horrified, and by the time my dadi ji arrived, it was all over. Our father and others all took it in stride. There was no investigation, no coroner, no nothing. He had a family, which I believe included ten children. He was the breadwinner. We felt guilty somehow, like we failed him because he died in our house, waiting for my dadi ji. We thought the family would be angry at us and blame us. We were anxious about seeing them all. We were amazed that not only did they not blame us or question anything we did, but they also felt a special bond with us since we were present during their loved one's death. This was the first death I had witnessed in my life that all of us siblings experienced. The reaction to and process of the death by the family and community was nothing that we expected. Just a day in the life of people who saw these things, and death, since no one was shielded from it. It was simply a part of life.

We travelled to many places around the country and saw the most beautiful temples hidden in the mountains. Some had monkeys running about, and some had bats. Others were in the middle of nowhere, and the only thing we saw on the route, were lots of vultures sitting on trees waiting for, what? Something or someone to die. Oh, please don't let it be one of us! There was always a chance the vehicle we were on would break down. There were no shops or gas stations close by and certainly no BCAA to call even if cell phones had been in use at that time. People relied on one another, and somehow with a wire here, and a makeshift part there, people would make things work.

Our dadi ji was the perfect guide since he knew every temple ever erected and could tell the history of each and what event it was famous for. Like the well near the Golden Temple in Amritsar (Jallian Walla Bagh), where the British army opened fire on the people killing many women and children. This was depicted in a scene in the movie *Gandhi*.

Learning About Dadi ji and Respect

During these travels, we visited long-lost relatives or close friends of my parents. People had not seen our family since we left India. Dadi ji had left in 1959 and the rest of us in 1962. Most people visit regularly or sponsor relatives in Canada, but this was not the case in our family. Everyone we met had great respect for my father, and it was the first time I realized that he was considered a great man. The fact that he had remained so humble and lived so modestly (frugally, we called it) was of inspiration to the people who knew him. They knew the stories of people leaving India, only to lose their way, becoming focused on material wealth and competing to show who had more than the other. They would raise children who knew nothing of their culture, language, or showing respect towards their parents and elders. In this regard, we realized that we had become those children.

In India, we often challenged in an argumentative tone something Dadi ji said. He had become accustomed to this and said nothing. People set us straight quickly, chastising us for speaking to our dadi ji in a disrespectful manner by questioning him or his direction. As time passed, it became evident that our dadi ji was a revered man and was considered a sacred person due to his writings and knowledge of the Sikh faith, and his principles and how he lived his life and treated others. I, too, began to understand and respect him in a similar way, though he never treated his family any differently. But regardless of status, children are raised to always respect their elders and obey their instructions. I never forgot this and have always gone to the aid of any elderly in need.

Nowhere did this reverence of our dadi ji become more evident than when we arrived in Amritsar, Punjab. The holiest place for the Sikh people. This is where the famous Golden Temple is located, and this too was featured in the *Gandhi* film. But it also got international news coverage when Indira Gandhi ordered the army to invade the Golden Temple to root out so-called "terrorists." Sikhs who believed in an independent state of Punjab had formed the Khalistan movement, and the army decided they were a threat to national security. The holy temple was attacked, desecrated, and many people were killed. This led to the assassination of Indira Gandhi (no relation to Mahatma Gandhi).

Apparently, during the British withdrawal and the impending separation and forming of a new country, Pakistan, the Sikhs had also voiced their desire for separation from India, to form their own country or independent state of Punjab. The understanding between the parties was that this was to be supported but delayed until after the separation of Pakistan to limit the massive changes and movement of people India would already be undergoing. This never happened; therefore, these sentiments resurface from time to time. Punjab is a resource-rich state, providing most of the water and power to the predominantly Hindu population. The Sikhs are considered to be the most industrious and successful people who also have the largest agricultural lands providing wheat and rice for export. They are the backbone of the country. However, being a very small minority, the people of Punjab rightly feel their state is not receiving fair treatment or allocation of services or other resources that are proportionate to what they provide the rest of the country. In fact, in 2021, at this writing, there are mass protests by the Punjabi farmers against the unfair practices against them and their livelihood. The government has responded with violence and arrests, even though the protests and marches are peaceful. The Sikhs have a history of fighting to the death for their principles. They are warriors and defenders of justice, and the future for them in India is in question.

Corruption in the Indian government was legendary and is not much better today. Taxes that are paid rarely go back into infrastructure or desperately needed programs. Adults did not just get to move out on their own. That simply was not an option financially. Social systems and traditions filled the gap. Most women were given minimal access to education. A woman never lived on her own. She moved from the family home to her husband's home (that of her in-laws) as soon as she was married. Conversely, a son would remain in his own home, and his wife would raise the children and look after her in-laws into their old age.

The gap between the rich and the poor was extreme. At that time, there was no middle class. People were generally destitute, poor, or rich beyond comprehension. India had a ruling class. Rajas (kings) ruled the country, and wealth was not distributed fairly or equally. Even after India became independent from British rule, becoming the world's largest democracy, the masses did not have access to a better life. This has changed over the decades, and there is a thriving economy and a robust tech industry. Most people, including women, are much more educated. People routinely own cars, TVs, cell phones and AC if they want it. The economy has improved substantially, although overpopulation remains a significant problem. Government corruption continues to thwart India's progress in development domestically in terms of lack of infrastructure for huge areas in India. There is a lack of financial assistance in general for the disabled or seniors.

Some areas are pristine and well maintained. Other areas have open sewage and very few municipal services to keep the streets clean. Foreign investment and development projects are also seriously impacted by corruption and impenetrable bureaucracy. Things move at a snail's pace, and the delays cost more in time and money. There were a number of developers from Germany that talked about this during one of my many subsequent visits to India.

India is vast, diverse, and full of contrast and paradox: elaborate religious structures of gold and marble are surrounded by cardboard shacks and people begging, some blind or without limbs. The sounds, smells, and the sheer number of people were all overwhelming and, at times, exhausting. The hustle and bustle of the streets was constant, the sound of horns always blaring. Conversely, other areas were less chaotic and seemed very serene. With little electricity used in these areas, the sky revealed stars I had never seen in my life. It was the most brilliant, beautiful sight to behold. It looked truly magical. There was not a single square inch in the sky not shining brightly with stars. After this, I never understood why we looked at fireworks. They are noisy and polluting. Nothing can match the absolute beauty and magic of nature.

Stars in the sky.

Having travelled all across India, we arrived at Amritsar, and it felt like home to Dadi ji. People worshipped him. They knew he was deeply spiritual and wise. He was humble. He was generous. Never an air of superiority over anyone, despite his immense accomplishments as a self-taught man who literally travelled the world and was revered everywhere. No one ever wanted my father to leave once they had spent time with him. People wanted to be in his presence and to serve him. He literally had to leave a suitcase with some belongings as assurance that he would be back, or people would not let him leave. His fate was truly amazing since the love people had for him saved his life on several occasions. He recalled an occasion when visiting in Iran (I believe) where he and a friend decided they wanted to see a movie the following day. But another person was insistent that he come to their home for dinner. No matter how many stories Dadi ji made about why he could not attend, the man would not take no for an answer. Just to appease him, Dadi ji said "fine" but had no intention of going. The man agreed to pick him up for dinner the following day at a designated time. My dadi ji and his friend intended to be gone to the movie by then, but for some reason, the man came early to pick Dadi ji up. Now he could not leave for the movie. The following day, it was reported that a terrorist attack occurred that very night at the very theatre he was going to be in. The attendees were locked in, unable to leave, while the perimeter was gassed and set ablaze. The love of others saved him. My dadi ji had hundreds of such examples. It was no different in Amritsar. They did not want Dadi ji to leave. He was a global icon in many ways, and they had not met anyone with his particular status and accomplishments. Therefore, it was unanimous that Dadi ji be nominated for the position of Singh Sahib, a title reserved for this high-level appointment at the Golden Temple. Dadi ji had never planned to pursue such a goal and was very honoured. This is such a rare, coveted position that he had to accept the opportunity to do service here. There was a huge ceremony that lasted a few days with honours, rituals like an inauguration.

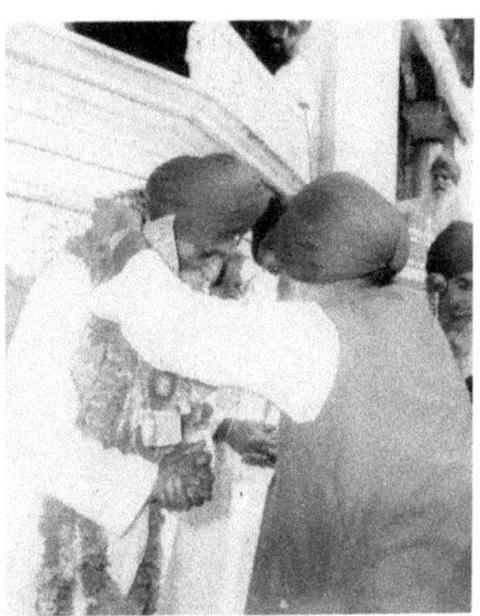

Dadi ji's inauguration of his appointment as Garanthi (Priest) at the Golden Temple.

Dadi ji would subsequently be appointed the highest position within the Sikh religion as Head Garanthi (Priest). By comparison, it would be equivalent to the Pope in the Vatican.

I have a magical image etched in my memory of this temple in Amritsar. One night, from our rooftop, we had a clear view of the Golden Temple (Sri Harmandir Sahib). Looking out at the beautiful site, suddenly, as it often did, the power went out. For a few seconds, it was a total blackout. But the temple had its own generator. When that was turned on, the only thing that was visible was the beautiful temple shining in complete darkness. Its image mirrored in the perimeter of water with the biggest, brightest moon I had ever seen. I felt the spirit, and specialness of this temple, in this place. I would revisit here many times in the future, and the feeling from that occasion remains. I can sit on the cool marble floors, look, and listen to the live performance of hymns (kirtan) and be transported into a peaceful, harmonious place. There were always many people, almost twenty-four hours a day doing service (sava), serving fresh, cold water, cleaning, cooking, and serving food for free to anyone. Currently, the temple feeds up to 100,000 people a day. It is of no cost to anyone, regardless of race, religion, or culture. It is referred to as God's kitchen (langar), and this occurs in every Sikh temple around the world. The generosity of the Sikhs is truly remarkable and humbling.

The Golden Temple in Amritsar.

Brother Paul in front of Golden Temple.

Volunteers preparing and serving langar at Golden Temple.

Another profound memory involves yet another blackout in Amritsar. We were out in the local market in the evening, looking to purchase some clothing. Suddenly, the power went out. No one panicked. All the shop owners and street vendors lit candles and carried on, "business as usual." One had no idea how long the power would be out for. Two minutes, hours, or days? We felt unsafe (justified or not) and bolted out of the shop. In the dark, we could no longer make out the landmarks to guide us back to our home. By luck, fate, "divine intervention," or whatever, we recognized a man who lived beside our residence. We followed him home because he knew exactly how to navigate himself in complete darkness. You see, he was blind.

Arwinder on roof top near Golden Temple.

Another surreal experience was the music we listened to while in India, particularly in Amritsar, which is where we lived for the longest duration. The only cassette tapes my brother had brought from England were the debut album by Santana, the debut album by Led Zeppelin, the album by America, *A Horse with no Name*, and Jethro Tull's, *Thick as a Brick*. These were blared at full volume, but no one complained, even with the high-pitched screams in some of the Led Zeppelin songs. One of the locals danced to Santana and found it very enjoyable.

Another such experience was also in Amritsar. We were walking through the market and happened across a van with a couple (hippies) that were travelling and living in their van. They were white people! We were so excited to speak to people in English. Incredulously, they were from New Westminster, our hometown. We talked up a storm, and every time I glanced around, there was a growing number of spectators. I overheard some of them debating about what language we were speaking. It sounded unfamiliar because we were speaking so quickly and fluently (dressed in Punjabi dress). The crowd became huge, and we had become completely surrounded. We suggested to people they perhaps could carry on, but we were too curious for them to break away. We eventually left but were happy to speak to "our" people from back home. It was a sign that we were becoming very homesick.

One thing that strikes me as a contrast between the "West" and other countries is not ever hearing anyone in India tell white people, some living there and even begging, to "Go back to your country," or "Stop speaking English; speak our language if you want to live here." It would never occur to people to expect such a thing or suggest it. Foreigners were left to live and let live.

We began wondering about our life from here on. I could see how totally fulfilled and content Dadi ji had become. He never came here with the goal in mind of remaining in India once again, serving as priest. But due to the overwhelming respect and love by the people, he embraced his new destiny. His numerous books about the Sikh teachings and other philosophical, spiritual writings had been published and would be widely used by religious-based schools in India and abroad.

Not only did the community worship my dadi ji, but people also worshiped us, his children. Strangers would kneel down to touch our feet as a sign of respect for our father. We could understand our father being revered, but this was very unexpected and foreign treatment for us, and it made us feel uncomfortable and undeserving of it.

Marriage or Escape

We became increasingly aware that time was running out. Having settled into a permanent life now in Amritsar, as it seemed, the members of the community began pressing Dadi ji to start looking for a suitable husband for my sister and a possible engagement for me. Nothing was discussed about our brother Paul, who was older than me. I saw what life was like for the women around me. Though many were happy, loving families, it was clear what the division of duties was and that most revolved around marriage, having children, and caring for the household and others. Things we valued, like having an education or career and self-autonomy and independence, were not in the equation, and a life of servitude made our hearts heavy, and our concerns of an arranged marriage were becoming a valid issue. Our dadi ji was well aware of how difficult it was for Mom and him to have a successful marriage, and he was not inclined to put us in that situation. Unlike Mom, we had been raised in Canada and being the subservient, dutiful wife was nothing short of horrifying for us. Almost daily, adults would bring pictures of their children or other extended family members and would discuss the possible union and that they were open to their son moving back to Canada with us. My mom's words rang loudly in my ears now. I understood why she had made comments about marriage and the duties of being a wife and mother when it was not your choice or a union of your own choosing. It hit me like a bolt of lightning, and it brought it into my reality. I could see how frightening even the thought of it was to us. How were we going to be able to exercise that choice?

Dadi ji was now *the* leader of the Sikh faith, and he could hardly openly express how we were feeling. He had to appease the community, which was quite a forceful and vocal group of people; it was clear we needed an exit strategy and the sooner, the better.

The problem was that since leaving Canada about two years ago, we had lost contact with our mother. She had no idea where we were, and we had no information about her whereabouts. Dadi ji understandably was not comfortable putting us on a plane to an uncertain situation. After all, we were all just kids ranging from about six or seven to about twenty-one or two. Aside from this obstacle, Dadi ji did not have enough money to purchase tickets to travel from India to Canada, so the chances of getting out of India and the potential trap of marriage (as we saw it) were looking bleak.

My sister and I talked about various scenarios and going straight to Canada was out of the question. The only possible scenario was to go back to England. We were well supported by the Sikh community there, and we had lived and worked there for a year prior to arriving in India. So why not go back in the same manner?

Questions Dadi ji asked we could now answer. Yes, the community would take us in and help with a place to stay. Yes, we would have money to live by working in the factories as we had before, and this would enable us to earn money to purchase the tickets to go on to Canada. Before then, we could track Mom down and let her know where we were and of our plan to return to her. She would have time to put things together as well. When we got back to Canada, our plan would be to complete our education, and we knew Dadi ji was always keen and dedicated to us getting an education.

Dadi ji still had reservations, but this was a plan that he could support. He knew about the level of support we would get in England, so we were not going into an unknown situation, and he knew we could get jobs very easily as well. Most importantly, he also knew that time was running out for us in regard to matrimonial issues, and it was now or never. The only major obstacle was getting Dadi ji to agree to let Nina go with us. He was vehemently opposed to letting Nina go, as she was too young to be working, and he and Nina had become so attached, bonded so deeply, that he did not think he could just let her leave. He would be heartbroken as they had been inseparable since the day, we joined him in England. Dadi ji used to recount how many nights he had cried himself to sleep, and anytime he heard the sound of a baby, he would think of Nina and would be devastated that she was not with him. Now that they had been closer than ever before, he did not think he could survive the separation. Nina, too, would be heartbroken as Dadi ji was her whole world. Her sense of security and attachment would be severed, but we knew that being young, she would adjust. Again, we had to make a case for Nina by focusing on her education since none of us had been attending school since coming to India.

To this day, I can't imagine the strength and immense love it took for Dadi ji to put us all, but especially Nina, on the plane and say goodbye. That selfless act was proof of how deep his love was, the ability to let go, to make the ultimate sacrifice for the sake of one's children. Dadi ji most likely cried himself to sleep every night, but we were elated as we prepared to leave India to a path that would bring us closer to our dream and hope of returning to Canada, a country we only now realized we were so blessed to be living in. We felt a sense of immense gratitude to our parents for bringing us to Canada, and an appreciation for the high standard of life we enjoyed, but most important of all was to live in a country that allowed us, especially women, to make our own decisions and be in control of our destiny. The fact that this was the first time that concepts like independence and freedom were being analyzed and appreciated was, in itself, a privilege. One that a vast number of people in the world did not enjoy.

THE GREAT ESCAPE

Departure India/Arrival England

Deportation, Detention, and Rescue

That was how it came to be that we were on an airplane headed to England once again. With no concrete plans in place and no guardians, we arrived at Heathrow Airport without a care in the world. That would all change in a matter of a few minutes when we were told something crucial that we had totally forgotten, consciously or not, that would cause us some complications now. As mentioned above, before we had left for India, Dadi ji's contacts in England had taken care of business such as getting his visitor's visa extended during his stay in England but not ours.

Upon arrival at Heathrow once again, we were excited to begin our life as we had before: to stay with the Sikh community, work at a factory, and make money to buy tickets to return permanently to Vancouver, Canada. When we were confronted with the fact that all of us, the same "suspects" that had been in England illegally for six months prior, had been warned we would have problems if we ever tried to re-enter the UK, well, here we all were again. In the even worse situation of having no money or parent. We did not have acceptable answers to satisfy the official and he may have understandably concluded we were intentionally disobeying the laws and warning about returning. He promptly informed us that we were being denied entry to the country. The protocol, as is the case everywhere, is to be "returned to the country of origin." That meant India. He had no idea how we had barely managed to leave India and make it this far, on route to our actual destination, Canada. We had no money to pay for tickets to Canada. Since we were Canadian citizens, we would have been allowed to transit through, but without financial means, they had no option.

We were placed in the "detention centre" sort of jail or "holding cells." We were not in cells, but in a place that had rooms to sleep, and meals would be brought to us. There was only one other detainee, a male person from Iran. We were not separated from each other. We would sit at mealtime and watch TV, but we were locked in and could not leave at all. They were going to allow us thirty-six to forty-eight hours before deporting us back to India. Our hearts sank, knowing if that happened, we would not be able to leave India, and the time for marriage could no longer be avoided. We could not even imagine this as our fate.

With the phone contact of the Sikh temple president where we had resided previously, we made a plea. He had no idea we had arrived, but after hearing our desperate situation, he quickly made calls and rounded up enough support from the community (they had such reverence for our father and us) to purchase airfare to Toronto, Canada. Did we know anyone there? No. It did not matter. It was Canada, and that was home and freedom.

Immediately from total despair, we were at once elated. *We were going home!* It was a win-win situation. The authorities did not have to worry about what to do with us or pay for our return to India. We did not really want to be in the UK. It was our only means to an end. Now we did not have to worry about staying and working (illegally) again. The amazing generosity of the Sikh community was paying for airfare once again. As always, they were there to help us in any way we needed. Truly remarkable. Our father had no idea we had been denied entry and were in "detention" in the UK and that soon all four of his children would be on a plane headed to Toronto where we knew no one. We knew we had one connection no matter where in the world we went, the Sikh community.

HOME SWEET HOME

Departure England/Arrival Canada

Upon landing at the Toronto airport, I literally kissed the ground. I was bursting with gratitude and joy, and I am certain I was happier at this moment than if I had won a ten-million-dollar lottery. This was the biggest lottery win of my life, and it was truly a defining moment. We had five British pounds. We asked the local taxi driver—yes, South Asian—to transport us to the nearest Sikh temple, and that is exactly where we arrived. All four of us, no money, and suitcases in hand.

Upon arrival, we had to track our contacts down. A mutual family friend informed my mother of our situation. She, of course, had no idea we were arriving. She had to borrow money to purchase train tickets from Toronto to Vancouver. Meanwhile, our father had no idea of the drastic turn of events and the world trek adventure all his children had been on, including a stint in "jail." We learned after Mom was on her own, she could not make payments, and the house was repossessed. Our beloved home that I still have dreams about.

We had left Canada suddenly to go to the UK, not knowing how long we would be there before we embarked on our trip to India. Once we arrived in India, we had no idea how long we would be living there. We were ready to return to Canada, as we were home sick. Since our father was remaining there permanently, as far as we could see, and the "marriage clock was ticking," we had to make our big escape. We had no way of knowing what would transpire. It appears unpredictability had become our way of life. This was sort of the grand finale of the two-year adventure.

Our father learned from the Sikh president what had happened and about our departure to Toronto. Regardless of all the obstacles and many remaining, he was relieved for us. I am sure, not nearly as much as we. Our travels never seemed routine, as we returned from England as quickly as we had left.

The theme of certain situations being like winning a lottery would become a lifelong perspective that helped me revisit those lotteries that have nothing to do with money. These are worth more than all the money in the world. I would go back to this well for the rest of my life to remind myself how many lotteries I had already won and would continue to win. This allowed me to be grateful and appreciate the lotteries that others would not even consider as such. I include the lottery of good health, having all my limbs. The lottery of emotional and psychological well-being, having all my senses. What a gift it is to be able to taste, smell, see, hear, touch, and speak. The lottery of living in Canada. Of feeling joy and happiness. Lottery of freedom, choices, and independence.

The train took about two days, if I recall. Nina had motion sickness, but we finally arrived, after two long years, at home in Vancouver. Mom was there to pick us up and seemed truly happy to see us again. The time to herself seemed to be good for her.

There was one more ironic cultural shift. We came back wearing saris, and Mom was dressed in a big flowery dress and wore a floppy hat. She had become a hippy during our time away.

This early childhood transition, coupled with my life-changing journey by 1974, left me aware that I was quite different from most people my age. Our extensive travels throughout India were very impactful at such a critical, impressionable age. Seeing and experiencing the harsh realities of extreme poverty and disparities in standards of living was shocking. How limited people were to control their destiny was something I had not given much thought to until I had the chance to see it firsthand.

I also saw for the first time that nothing could be wasted, or considered waste, in daily life, such as the geckos eating flies and the numerous scorpions in the outhouses. I was impressed by how humans also had to make use of any available resource, like the children who collected the cow dung and slapped them into flat discs to use as fuel for cooking with fire. Those cows also provided milk and related foods such as cream, yogurt, and cheese, for example. Their contribution to survival was obvious in people's daily lives. Everyone knew where their food came from. It was better to allow the animals to live out their lives rather than kill them for food, which would only provide meat for an extremely limited time and for few people.

Due to financial hardship and overpopulation, people did not have the luxury of living based on individual needs and certainly not desires. No one received any kind of social assistance or aid of any sort.

Living in India, a world drastically different in every way, was surreal and extremely enlightening. It was the best education of my life. I describe it as a "tour of duty." Returning to Canada two years later, I was no longer the same person that had left. I had learned many important life lessons that led me to paths very much my own. What others my age took as important, to me appeared petty or frivolous. Many material things were not as necessary as most people thought. In fact, I became very aware of the important difference between "needs" and "wants." Most things in Canada, from my experience, were wants. We had all our basics: a place to live, food to eat, clean water, and clean air. Everything else was a bonus, not a necessity for survival. Therefore, it was not worth fussing about not having it. I learned what I needed to be satisfied and happy was much less than what others around me needed.

In Canada, there were warehouses crammed with food. Free medical. Hospitals and ambulance services twenty-four hours a day. The streets were clean and well maintained.

I also had a much more profound appreciation for another critical thing in my life, personal freedoms and choices. I had the ability to choose my destiny: attend school, choose a career, decide where to live, live independently, choose to be married or not, and whether to have children or not. These choices were something I had never given much thought to. Now that I saw what very well would have been my life, had it not been for immigrating to Canada, I realized how vital freedom was. How many people in the world had no access to basic needs, including personal freedoms and choices? Billions. This made me feel privileged, but not in the ways others did. Basic needs were the most important things to survive, but freedoms and choices allowed us to thrive. This revelation allowed me to have the happiness others did not. Sadly, they took these most vital things in their lives for granted. They missed the experience I had, did not learn what was important in life. What was a want, and what was a need? This deep awareness had a protective effect on me and my life. I was happy, satisfied, and grateful for everything I had. I knew I had an abundance in every aspect of my life. I had control over my destiny. How much is this worth? Many wealthy and famous people feel trapped because they lose their simple freedoms. Being able to leave their house, sit in a park, go to a store freely, as others do. But they have lost that, and their wealth never seems worth the cost.

Many never seem to achieve happiness, regardless of how much they attained, how hard they worked, how many material things they collected, or how many times they married or how many kids they had. A true inner sense of happiness or contentment often eluded them.

Teens my age complained about what they perceived others had (better clothes, more money, more privileges, and more independence or freedom), all the while having no appreciation for the fact, they had these and even more important things. Here, teens complained about "having" to attend school (free of cost), move out on their own, get a job, not having a car, and countless other things. In other places in the world, girls begged and dreamed of going to school, some walking miles every day. Others were actually killed for trying. Teens here have personal space. They have freedoms like choosing which clothes to wear. In many cases (men and women) in India must get married, and often not to a person of their choosing. They have to have children and live with their parents, even after marriage. There is no disrespecting elders, and one has to follow their direction.

During our stay in India, the locals were offended that we would openly disagree with our father, or we simply did not want to do something. Until then, I had not thought that this too was a privilege not afforded to many. My respect for elders remained with me, and I could never speak rudely to an elderly person nor ignore them if they needed help. Elders have earned that minimum privilege by virtue of the time they have lived and what they have seen and experienced over their lifetime. It distresses me to see someone mistreat an elderly person. Well, children and animals too.

I was considered very mature for my age, and I had a serious, reflective aspect of my nature. I questioned things and needed to make sense of people and the world around me. I had a philosophical perspective towards life, people, and problems.

ACKNOWLEDGING MY MENTORS

As a young child, I was hungry for wisdom and knowledge. I always felt most comfortable with people twenty to thirty years my senior. They recognized that need in me and took me under their wing. I am grateful for the amazing mentors I have had in my life. Though most have left this earth, their influence and guidance in my life remains powerful and eternal. They are worthy of my gratitude and mention.

My father was the first person who taught me about having strong convictions and living by principles and with integrity. As a religious person in the Sikh faith who was respected around the world for his contributions and spiritual writings, Dadi ji's spiritual presence become deeper as he aged. He never stopped marvelling at how amazing nature was, how birds would all fly in formation without hitting the other, how brilliant were the colours of flowers, birds, and aquatic life. That regardless of species, "as babies, they were always cute." He had no fear of death. In fact, he had a sense of peace and comfort about it. His eyes were always filled with so much love and gratitude that nothing needed to be said. He was so appreciative of everything. He referred to all females that cared for him (even me) as "good baby" no matter how old we got. At the care home the last year or so, he would sometimes think he was in a gurdwara (Sikh temple), as people often revisit early experiences. He would announce with amazement that he was given meals three times a day! Sometimes he would get offended if they did not bring me a tray because, in Langar (God's kitchen), everyone is supposed to be brought food. A couple of incidents were quite amazing. I have heard that some people can see and communicate with deceased loved ones. I witnessed this numerous times with Dadi ji. I was outside his room and could see no one else. He was sitting up on the bed saying, "Pass me my socks." When I entered, he said, "Oh good, did Mom visit with you?" He was going to speak to her again but asked, "Where did she go?" He even looked under the bed to make sure she was not there!

I said, "But Dadi ji, she died a long time ago."

Then he would get annoyed and say, "Fine, let her do what she wants to do then!"

It was hilarious, but I don't think he believed me that she died and would get annoyed that she did not come to visit the kids. I think his spiritualty was so deep that he made these connections. He was not confused, did not have Alzheimer's, he was totally coherent and actually was in and out of another realm. Totally awake. Reading the book *Final Gifts* by Maggie Callanan and Patricia Kelly, hospice nurses working in palliative care, give me an amazing amount of helpful information. It was written, so loved ones and caregivers can help people through their end-of-life journey. I learned it is important not to argue or dismiss their experience and needs. People ask questions or request certain things to prepare for their final journey. My dad was so angry and frustrated because he was all dressed in a suit and had a briefcase beside him. He was relieved when I came and said, "Good you're here. I have been asking them all day when the train is coming, and no one is telling me." He was in a panic and did not want to miss the train. He had been sitting in this area (not in his ward) all day. I had to relieve his panic by giving him believable information and evidence. I said, "Dadi ji, the train is cancelled today."

"OK."

He came back into his room. Then he wanted to know how to get the key to get into his place when he arrived there. I told him that they would leave the door open for him. This satisfied him. Then he asked where the ticket for the train was. I pulled out a receipt from the store, a plain white thin slip of paper. He took it and, after looking at it closely, threw it down, annoyed, saying that was not it. Luckily, I had a small book of postages that had the right size, feel, and colours that resembled it better. Relieved, he took it and, satisfied, he put it in the inside pocket of his jacket. I was surprised that staff in this particular place either did not know or care to take a few minutes to do this. It calms the person down and allows them to be more at peace once the questions are answered. If they did not get this training, it should be mandatory. Next time saw Dadi ji, that incident was forgotten, and it would be uneventful. When the next such event occurred, I would do the same. But if I had not seen him every day, he would have endured unnecessary worry, anxiety, and suffering—no reason for this to happen to a loved one.

I recall visiting Dadi ji daily in the hospital after he had a stroke years before he passed away. As I was leaving, I walked near an elderly woman, and she grabbed my arm tightly and locked her eyes with mine. I remained looking into her eyes. She said nothing, but I could see fear or terror in her eyes. I slowly began to dislodge my arm and tried to comfort her as I left. I tried to let the nurse know she might need something. I felt bad for leaving as she did not seem to have anyone with her.

When I returned the next day, I did not see her. She had passed away. I now realize she knew she was dying and needed someone to be with her. I wish I had known this as a sign that she was at the very end of her life. I regretted I did not know enough to have stayed with her. I so wish I had been there for her. It was sad to see a person so alone despite having many people around her. I was grateful that, for whatever reason, she sensed that she could literally reach out to me. It was such a small moment yet so significant. It does not take much time or effort to be there for someone, even a stranger. Pay attention, don't just walk by people. Make eye contact. See them. Feel them.

I will always remember seeing Dadi ji at a visit to the second care home he went to. It was beautiful and had lots of windows and plants. He was smiling and happily singing. The staff said he had been signing like this since he woke up. When asked what he was singing about, he said, “I am going to a wedding.” My father had performed many weddings in his lifetime. But this union, he continued, “was going to be between the moon and a star.” That beautiful idea and vision filled my heart with tremendous happiness. I felt so close to my father at this time and loved hearing him speak in his joyous, almost childlike way. He always embraced the natural world. It seemed like he was going back to being a part of it. His death was as spiritual as his life, and that gave me much comfort and eased the loss of his passing, though only slightly. I miss him, his smile and sense of humour, every day. Maybe it is no coincidence that my father’s first book was a book of maxims, as is this one. And much of what I honour, and advocate is for the natural world that he cared so deeply about. Maybe this is the only way people become immortal. Not their bodies, but their essence and knowledge, carried through the generations.

Dadi ji spiritual leader, philosopher, and writer.

Fidel visiting Dadi ji in care home.

My mother and father were very opposite in personalities and priorities. My mother always wanted to be a free spirit. From her, I learned that women have their own hopes and dreams that may have nothing to do with a domestic life. That having control over our own destiny was not available to everyone and should never be taken for granted. That what others expected of you or said was your "duty" was not for them to decide. This was unbelievably valuable for me to be aware of at such an early age. I became more aware of freedoms that only came from making very conscious choices.

Mom playing sitar.

Mom in India before immigrating to Canada.

Lawrence Anthony (Tony) Potts, I met at age ten when he moved into our family home in New Westminster as a tenant. We remain in contact fifty-three years later. He was an airline pilot when I first met him. His career included delivering supplies to remote locations, like Papua New Guinea. The flight path and conditions were treacherous, and the locals were known to have practiced cannibalism, albeit not for many decades. He had a positive experience and returned many times. Prior to this, Tony was a master marine in the British Merchant Navy. When he retired, he was a senior officer in the search and rescue division of the coast guard in Richmond, BC. Tony lived all over the world and had the most amazing stories to tell. He was also the first feminist (and male) I had ever met. He was concerned about animal rights, ecology, and the human impact on the planet. He was particularly good at modelling the importance of not being wasteful, littering, or using harmful substances. I do not recall what year, but he had moved out to live in

Richmond, a city less than an hour away. Meanwhile, I had been away for my two-year travel to England and India.

Arwinder shorty after arriving back in Canada after 2 years abroad.

I recall feeling like I was on cloud nine, even after our plane landed back in Canada. I was home. Regardless of what would happen next (the future was a total mystery), nothing could go wrong while living in the best country on the planet. Sadly, throughout life, I would learn that many people took this most precious place for granted, even complained about it when they had nothing to compare it to. That would upset me deeply. But for now, I was back home, filled with boundless optimism.

With education being the priority, I found an accelerated high school program that was available at a community college. This would allow me to complete Grades 9 to 12 in one year. That was an obvious choice, and it would be as though there had been almost no interruption in school attendance at all. In 1976, I had completed Grade 12. Before, school had been of minimal interest to me, but now my enthusiasm for learning and obtaining a formal education was motivation. This was the next step in completing my self-discovery, self-development, and growth. I had the additional life experience of my travels abroad, and life could not have been more positive and filled with anticipation.

With life being chaotic before my journey abroad, I moved and changed schools frequently. I had trouble with this as a young teen, never fitting in due to ethnicity and being new to school. We are also given the green light to miss school since our family did live shows performing Indian dance and music. Mom, more than Dadi ji, wanted to pursue this aspect of life. Dadi ji loved it too but not if it interfered with formal education for the children. I was behind my grade level in high school and had little interest in school. It was probably the best thing to have left school to travel for two years. When I returned as a mature person dedicated to learning, I discovered I was smart and quite capable of learning quickly and successfully. I always shared this with parents when they voiced concerns about their teenager's lack of school attendance or progress. That time can be made up when the person is more ready and willing to do so. It is time and effort better spent. The other priority after returning to Canada was reconnecting with Tony. He was living in an area in Richmond referred to as "Steveston." He shared property with his close friends, Gordon and Bianca Barnes. Tony introduced me to them, and there was an immediate connection. They, too, became mentors. They were staunch feminists and ecologists. They were all well-read, informed people.

The Silent Spring, by Rachel Carson, had been published in 1962. It was ground-breaking scientific research and extremely shocking. People learned how harmful and lethal chemicals and pesticides were. Commercially, DDTs and pesticides were treated as a miracle cure and used in all kinds of applications in daily lives. From spraying them on crops to "protect" human food from so-called predators like insects and birds to spraying them on soldiers to kill lice. The effects on humans were seen by a rise in various forms of cancers as well as negative effects on fetus health and development. The destruction to wildlife, plants, and animals was devastating, as it would be to the whole ecosystem for generations to come. There was a tremendous backlash against Rachel Carson and the book, partly because it was authored by a woman, but more importantly, it was critical of an industry. Any threat to an industry's potential for unlimited commercial growth and profit was met with hostility and disdain. In 2021 things are no different. In fact, worse since corporations have become much more powerful financially and politically. Any time facts reveal harmful effects of human action, particularly involving the corporate world, the attacks against the information and "messenger" are immediate and severe. The industry is fully aware of the risks and harm caused. The public concerns are legitimate and scientifically proven, but corporations spend billions of dollars defending their industry rather than paying out one dollar in "compensation." Those injured, suffering illness or death resulting from their products directly, or due to dumping toxic waste back into the environment, communities, and into homes are ignored, covered up, and considered collateral damage. "Profits before people or the planet" continues to be the mantra. At the age of seventeen, I was disturbed by these discussions, but they made me very aware that there were many unjust things happening in the world, and it was important to be aware and get involved. Never to be apathetic.

Lest I leave the impression that my mentors only involved themselves in what people might think of as being "controversial" issues, I should share other aspects of their life. They had many interests. Tony and the Barnes shared a mutual passion: boat building. They all met when they lived on a property in an area of Richmond where many boat-building enthusiasts lived. Tony built a fifty-two-foot yacht, which he named Ambush. It would be capable of sailing around the world. He built it all the while working full-time with search and rescue in the coast guard. It took him almost thirty years. He did complete it, but by that time, he was no longer keen to sail around the world. He seemed to sabotage the sale to each prospective buyer, and there were not that many. Finally, when he decided someone was "worthy" of it, he sold his beloved Ambush to them. He still maintains a connection to the new owner to keep tabs on her.

Tony's boat Ambush.

The Barnes were building their sailboat, the thirty-eight-foot Adriana. Unlike most couples at this time, Bianca became the sole breadwinner as a graphic artist at UBC so that Gordon could retire from his job as a mechanical engineer. This way, he could dedicate the time needed to work on the boat. In between, of course, he was building other things as required on their property. After moving to Salt Spring Island, there were larger projects: renovations to the house or building a staircase or a work shed. No matter what he was working on, he made every part he needed. As a machinist, he would make nuts, bolts, and nails and cut or carve wood pieces or metal to his specifications. Gordon worked slowly and methodically as any perfectionist would. Bianca was very artistic as a filmmaker and photographer and documented the whole process in a film and a book, *Real-Time Boatbuilding* by Bianca and Gordon Barnes.

The Barnes boat Adriana in the making.

This project spanned many decades, but unlike most people, they had no concern about "finishing" it. This was not a necessary goal. The joy was in the process of building and sharing this with boat enthusiasts and future generations. They were keenly aware that projects such as theirs were a dying art form. The changing times make it unlikely people would ever dedicate their whole lives to something that could never pay for itself in terms of financial cost, nor the immeasurable cost in time and labour. They documented not only the actual construction of the sailboat but also created a journal detailing their day-to-day lives. It is amazing and delightful to read and see the boat and their lives in evolution.

They made many friends in the work shed, such as birds, spiders, cats, dogs, and a horse that lived with them on the property. They taught me to see insects as friends, not foes since they played an important role in the ecosystem and protected us from bugs, mosquitos, and disease. They would admonish me not to kill a spider or destroy its beautiful web. The web was the home built by the spider, it was how it got its food, and it was beautiful to look at. It was not harming us, and it had a right to live and raise its young just as we do. Every day our life was filled with gifts from nature. The Barnes had many fruit and nut trees. They used them in making all kinds of wonderful foods and wine. Nothing was wasted. They were the first people I knew, at least in city living, that were composting, recycling, and reusing. All things in the ecosystem were needed, and every effort was made to use only biodegradable and nontoxic items that could be put back into the ecosystem. Just as humans receive all we need from the ecosystem, so do other species. We all must put something back. The relationship with nature needs to be symbiotic and of mutual benefit and accessible to all.

Friends in work shed.

Another important mentor was E. Margaret Fulton, a real powerhouse. Some of her achievements and accolades include feminist, teacher, theorist of education, author, public speaker, an advocate of social and political reform, recipient of the Order of Canada, a Governor General's Award, and more than a dozen honorary degrees in recognition of her life's work.

To me, she was one of the most humble people I knew, and she had a great sense of humour and infectious laugh, warm and affectionate. When Margaret retired, by chance she happened to relocate to the same area as Bianca and Gordon Barnes, on Salt Spring Island. I was extremely excited to introduce them to each other. It was no surprise they became best of friends. I now had four significant mentors in my life, and the five of us (Tony, Bianca, Gordon, Margaret, and me) were as close as anyone could be.

Tony, Arwinder leaving for trip to Clayoquot Sound.

Arwinder at Clayoquot Sound with amazing tree.

Margaret Fulton and Arwinder at Barnes home on Salt Spring Island.

Bianca, Gordon Barnes, Arwinder, Margaret in Salt Spring Island.

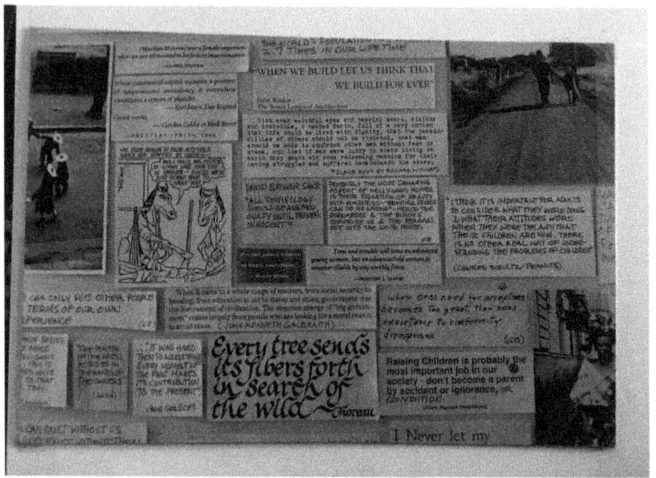

Hand made collage of maxims collected and sent as post card to Arwinder by the Barnes.

Me and one of my soul mates,
Fidel. Miss him everyday.

Current genius dog Monty. Detected cancer in Tony twice.

We all had extremely diverse backgrounds and origins, but we shared values, principles and followed similar paths in our lives. Tony and Margaret have remained single and childless by choice. Even though Gordon and Bianca had married, it was only due to outside pressures put on them by family (since it was very taboo to live together at that time). Both always resented this, and many decades later actually considered getting a divorce and "living together" just out of principle. But after over forty years of marriage, they decided it was not worth paying the legal fees to do so. But I understood the importance for them to live by their principles. Their life needed to reflect who they were, to align with their beliefs. They, too, were childless by choice. When people pressured them to have children, Bianca would simply say "We're waiting for a people shortage." That was just so refreshing to me. People who said, did, and lived as they chose, with no concern about fitting into the mainstream. People who lived by principles, truth, and without hypocrisy. I was a sponge taking it all in and learning lessons about being free-thinking, independent, challenging the status quo. Here were the most important adults (seniors) in my life, telling me that it is possible to go against the grain, not something to fear, but to embrace. They never locked themselves into a rigid model or fantasy of life. The people who followed the fantasy encouraged me to do what they were doing, but except for a few, they did not seem to be genuinely happy, at least not in the long term.

Conversely, my mentors were not telling me to live as they were, but I could see they were genuinely happy. They had no second thoughts or regrets about their choices. Nor did they feel they lacked anything. Unlike the horror stories I had heard, none of them had lives that were lonely, isolated, or without family or close, caring friends. They had so many people wanting their time and company that they had to place limits and restrictions on visits and social engagements. They were simply too busy. They were not sitting idly for people to drop by or visit. They pursued many important causes, hobbies, and interests in their lives. Their lives were full and meaningful. They had personal and financial freedoms others did not. I could see the differences between how they lived and how the mainstream lived, and these differences mattered immensely to me. I was taking notes and experiencing it all in real-time.

Interestingly, I knew as a teenager I was going to be childless by choice before I met most of my mentors. My choices in this regard were not influenced by them. But I felt validated for the first time in my life that my choices were totally appropriate, and more importantly, right for me. This was when I got the inkling that truths are universal. No matter place or time or difference in age, they remain constant. I realized that I felt comfortable with them because we shared certain truths and principles that were timeless. It did not matter how many decades apart in age we were; we were intimately connected. We did not have to explain ourselves to each other, though others often had many questions. I realized, being outside the mainstream was nothing like people would have us believe and fear. They were the most enthusiastic, inspirational people in my life. I was most comfortable and at peace being me, with them. There would be one more consequential mentor to arrive in my life. More on that later.

My mentors were pivotal in making me more observant, critically analytical, and reflective about the world and helped me clearly identify, with more conviction, my principles, values, and boundaries. These would guide me for the rest of my life. They also taught me that each person must search for their right path, that questioning and rebelling against that which was wrong was important and necessary. We need to use all our senses. Not just accept as truth what people say.

I also seemed to have a powerful connection with my friends and mentors. I can recall two such instances. The first involved an amazing prediction. I know others have had similar experiences, and some of the more powerful ones I have, I recall.

I have never watched soccer (football in Europe) nor had much interest. One night in 1998, I had a most vivid dream that France won the world cup. I knew the world cup was coming up and was to be hosted by France. I did not know what to make of it. I went to the seawall in Vancouver as I often did on a beautiful day.

While doing my run, I saw my good friend Paul Ygartua. He was often painting and selling his artwork there. In fact, his painting is featured on the cover of this book and his daughter, Tala, wrote the foreword. I finished my run and chatted with him, and he informed me the family would be leaving the next day to live in Paris, France, as they usually did every year. Intrigued about the timing of my dream, I shared this with Paul and suggested that he should do a painting of France winning the world cup. I added how amazing it would be for him to have done the painting in advance of their win, and it would be incredible and patriotic. Fans and art enthusiasts would not only be impressed with this prediction (the odds were astronomically low) but would be willing to pay lots of money to own an original of this historic occasion. He laughed it off, saying there were many teams that were favourites or in the running, but France was not one of them and had no chance. I begged, but, well, I am sad and disappointed that he did not take my advice. He and his family were in Paris while I watched along with the world as France did the impossible, beating Brazil (an odds favourite) 3-0. I could only imagine the frenzied crowd at that moment and how much they would have wanted such a painting. He probably could have had a bidding war and been a millionaire. Alas, it was not to be. I did not know if I could have placed a bet online or through other ways because if I had known how I surely would have.

Another similar event happened after I was at Margaret Fulton's apartment near UBC. She was excited about *Ishmael* and Daniel Quinn's other books, and she was helping me with ideas and gave me a contact who was going to interview me on a cable TV program about *Ishmael.* After our visit, I was walking down the stairs, and Margaret called my name. I had just walked outside, and the door had an automatic lock, so I could not come back in. She said, "I will call you at home." As I drove home, for some reason, I had one thought obsessively repeating in my head for the hour-long duration of the drive. I thought to myself that someone with Margaret's status and accomplishments would be a perfect person to get a reference letter from. She was my mentor and knew me and my character so well that I must ask her for this letter. I parked my car in the driveway, and as I entered my home, the phone was ringing. I picked it up, and it was Margaret. What she wanted to say to me as I was leaving was, "If you ever needed a reference letter, I would be happy to write one for you." Well, you can imagine our discussion about that. I can't explain it only that I have these often, and they are so precise it is uncanny. I learned that it was something very powerful and important to tap into and believe in.

My formal education in college and university fit easily with my nature. Read, question, study, research, analyze, debate, and come to an in-depth understanding of people and the world. I was invigorated by learning and seeking knowledge. My need to make sense of the world remained ingrained in my nature for the rest of my life. Like many others in University, I had no concrete objective or career goal. So, I took courses that interested me rather than pursue some obscure goal. Relying on my inner truth, on this occasion, turned out to be the correct path, as it always would. In 1977 I began attending Douglas College and went on to SFU.

Arwinder' s Graduation SFU.

DISCOVERING MY CALLING AND THE COMPASS

Cleary, my foundation of activism in causes such as peace, social justice, animal, and ecological rights took root during the times I spent with my mentors. I had developed the core of my character: who I am and what I believe. I also had a fierce passion for my principles that would not allow me to ignore any injustice or unethical conduct in my life, personal or professional. I was constantly taking injured birds to a sanctuary. Bringing people to safety—on one occasion, it was an elderly person wearing a housecoat, wandering in the middle of a street in freezing temperatures. The person was obviously confused and lost. I was appalled that car were just swerving around this person. I brought this person home, making her comfortable with hot tea and blankets and called the police. Her family was frantically searching for her. It only took a few minutes to prevent further suffering to the woman and her family. It upset me that people could ignore this.

I found people on a ski mountain that needed help. One man I accompanied down the mountain after he had taken a fall. He had vomited on the way down. I tried to enlist help from a ski patrol, but I think he was embarrassed and refused. At his suite, I called the hospital. They advised he needed to be monitored in case his condition worsened. I stayed until his friends returned after skiing, hours later. Another time, a child was standing, looking distressed, so I stopped. He needed assistance to make his way down the mountain. My friends were surprised that they never noticed so many people in need of help. Well, I was a new skier, and they were all whizzing by. But that was not the complete explanation. This happened too frequently, in various circumstances, to just be a coincidence. I had gained, for whatever reason, an extremely keen sense of observation of surroundings and people around me. Time and time again, I would come upon a situation, assess it, and ensure I did as much as possible to resolve it or hand it to someone who could. I could not just look the other way, hoping someone else would come along to help. I had to be able to sleep at night, and this was the only sure way I would. Later, it would become a source of fun at work because I often came to the office with another "stray," sometimes children, other times not.

I always worked to support myself while attending college and university. After graduating, I lacked direction on how to find a job, my mentor, Bianca, gave me the most simple and best advice. Use what you have that other don't. I said, "Well, my ethnicity and second language?"

She agreed. I soon was hired as a community worker for immigrants and refugees that required support and interpretation services. I never expected my interpreter and support role would become vital when visiting a pregnant South Asian immigrant woman expecting her first baby at Women's Hospital. She was utterly alone, having fled a domestic abuse situation. By chance, at this visit, I was informed that they had to "induce labour right now." I had no desire or intention of remaining for that! But the woman pleaded for me to stay, being terrified with no English skills. With a heavy heart, I had to stay. I could not abandon her at this moment. So, a bed was wheeled in for me in the delivery room, not that I got any sleep during the night with the frequent monitoring that had to be done. As she went into labour and until she got an epidural, she kept holding my hand tightly, repeating, "Don't ever have a baby." After the pain subsided, she relaxed, but I had to sit down and be given orange juice because I felt very woozy, like I might faint. Much later, she retracted her advice never to have a baby. She said it was ok to have one. I did not tell her I was not going to, regardless, as that was never in my plan.

Bianca was so right about using my particular traits, ones that others did not have, to find the right type of work. It was right on. She also taught me another important life lesson: if a relationship is not making you happy and fulfilled get out, and quick. Both people had to be equal partners and share a life, values, and interests, but they must also have their own interests and time outside the relationship for it to be healthy and last long term. She and Gordon even said, "Anytime one wants out, no questions asked." But when she was in her seventies, she said, "Well, now we might have a question or two." The other amazing thing Bianca and Gordon discussed early in their relationship was how they would deal with an affair by either one if it ever happened. They came to a mutual agreement on how they would, whether or not they wanted to know about it. They had a deep love and life commitment but did not want that to include jealousy, possession, or the idea of ownership. I have no idea if either one ever did, not that it would matter to me in the least. What I know is that they had a formula that was not imposed but was the most successful union between two people I have ever had the privilege to witness and experience over my forty years of knowing them. They truly did stay together until the day they passed away without ever saying those words to each other, nor did they want or need a hollow piece of paper to do so. Do it, not just say it. How many couples want the piece of paper that did not make the marriage last? How many have signed that paper numerous times in life? That should teach us something valuable right there. How you truly value, respect, and treat each other is an expression of love, not the words, not the piece of paper. That, too, was excellent advice.

During this time (1985-1986), I had an opportunity to go through the selection process for the Vancouver Police Department. They were seeking women, visible minorities, for the police force. Never having lifted a weight or run a block, I trained extremely hard to pass the physical. In Grade 8, I think it was, in gym class, we were all asked to do a sprint. I had no running shoes or gym wear. The teacher timed each of us individually with a stopwatch. I ran barefoot. The teacher stopped the watch, looked perplexed, and asked me to repeat it. Apparently, I was so fast that he doubted it was the correct time and had to verify it. I was always lean and flexible like rubber and could do all kinds of acrobatics. I did not realize until I was almost thirty, after training for the police department physical, that I had an extremely athletic body that was waiting for me to start utilizing it. I had overly broad shoulders, and as soon as I started working out, running, and swimming, it seemed as though my body responded quickly as though to say, "What took you so long?"

I received the highest score in my class for the eight-hour psychological evaluation. At this time, I was hired at the Vancouver Airport as a Customs and Immigration officer in preparation for the high volume of visitors to Vancouver for Expo 1986. It was "feast or famine." Either hundreds or thousands arrived simultaneously, or there would be no arrivals, resulting in downtime. The downtime allowed staff to build rapport and find ways to pass the time. I recall one manager asking me to "show my biceps" every time new people came around.

"The biceps" I was asked to show for fun.

After passing physical for Vancouver Police Department.

Arwinder as a Customs and Immigration officer at YVR during Expo 86.

I worked with many wonderful staff members and have fond memories of them. I had lots of interesting people, some celebrities and diplomats, pass through Primary Inspection. I learned of Americans beliefs about right to carry guns, as many Americans were shocked that guns, even for hunting, could not just be carried through. Often the stereotypical person (like hippies from Thailand) would get sent in for a further search in Secondary Inspection. Meanwhile, the well-dressed people with fancy suits and briefcases could have very expensive contraband. Some answers travellers gave to questions were hilarious. I had an item in hand that I shook, and I could hear something clinking around in it. I asked the person, "Do you know what's in here?"

The reply was, "I do, but I don't know how it got in there."

Obviously, this made no sense because they must have known how it got there if they knew what it was. No matter how many times I asked, it was the same answer. There was contraband in it, and they were charged the penalties to keep the item, or it would get seized.

This is an example of two lessons in life to add to our collection in our compass. If it does not make sense, does not add up, don't believe it. And there are people who will not tell the truth, even when faced with the facts and evidence to the contrary. Believe behaviour, not words. I am always amazed when people believe the person is truthful because they claimed to be.

There were times an elderly person had all their belongings removed from suitcases or packages. Even though I was told it was not our job to help repack it, I had to because of my respect for elderly people. I would accompany them out to make sure they saw their loved ones. I observed one thing that really surprised me: people bringing back things of little monetary value, but sentimental value became the most upset that the item could not be allowed into the country. The agriculture inspector (with the scent detection beagle) would take time to explain how bringing in a sausage from the UK could literally devastate our agriculture economy by introducing some parasite. Same with plants and vegetables. One person became so angry and hostile that we were accused of saving it to eat it later! We assured them it was going into an incinerator. Later, as a social worker, I recalled the anger seemed so disproportionate since I rarely got that extreme reaction when children had to be removed from parents. Perplexing indeed.

There was an option to apply for a permanent position, but again, my inner wisdom told me I had not yet found "my calling." I continued to pursue other paths.

In 1987, I began my lifelong career as a social worker, specializing in child protection and guardianship. This was a tremendously challenging career, spanning nearly thirty years. It was very much consistent with who I was as a person. Fate presented it, and I'm glad I jumped in with both feet.

I would need to bring forth all my education, experience, values, truths, boundaries and principles (my internal compass) to guide me through this complex work. Often, it felt like being in the midst of a tornado, as the work always involves conflicting needs or beliefs. It also shed light on how government and bureaucracies worked or didn't. Things that may appear simple and straightforward often become not. What seemed clear was suddenly derailed or filled with confusion or chaos—the roles and priorities different within one system. Something as simple as agreeing on who the "client" is, is amazingly not simple. Despite detailed manuals, directives, audits, and reviews stating the priorities, often people would find themselves at odds with one another and working against one another. Internal disagreements between individuals, offices, departments, regions and outside parties would use up the vital time and energy of a great number of people (resources) while the "clients" plight or future hung in the balance.

The job can involve logistical challenges. Relationships between staff and the great number of offices involved, differing styles, and individual strengths are bound to play a role. There is no doubt that child protection social work is about as complex as it gets. Unlike the ER, the risk, injury, and death may not be present, visible, or imminent. In child protection, there are many factors that come into assessing risk and level of risk. This may include history, but there may not be any. The tools provided are a guide, but they are open to some interpretation or subjectivity. So, one works less in "black-and-white" situations and more in the grey ones.

The greater the number of people involved in decision-making, the less a decision could be made. It would require an ever-growing number of levels and people to make the "final" decision, which could just be overturned sometimes due to pressure. This is crazy making for most of us that really care and want to do our best. Looking a child in the eyes, seeing and feeling their pain is important. That helps clarify what the priority is.

The skills required to be a social worker are vast and complex. One needs to manage huge caseloads, with varied client needs, excel at time management, and possess the ability to work with families of varying backgrounds and children of all ages. Being detailed at documenting and writing reports, making referrals, attending court, giving evidence, liaising with all disciplines and agencies, attending meetings, answering a barrage of incoming calls, visiting with clients and establishing trust with them (to name a few), all the while maintaining professional and personal boundaries is not something every single person can do. Some people work well with younger children, others with teens, others are good at time management, others with written work, and still others excel at conflict resolution. It is a lot to ask for and deliver. But the core of who we are is the only thing that might make the difference, especially when it really counts. I know, with out my "compass," it would have been near impossible to maintain the clear, steady, reliable inner strength that was needed.

THE COMPASS *is an internal tool, an ability to cut through the clutter and chaos to the exact truth, and the principle that must be applied to respond to it.*

This compass guided me through the chaos. This compass I could rely on, despite the conditions around me. This constant was present regardless of where I worked, the staff, the management team, and the working model since this changed many times over the decades. The optimum work conditions (anywhere) are where one has a strong, healthy, functioning, trustworthy, dedicated staff with a highly skilled and supportive supervisor(s) and management team. One can accomplish much, be more productive and effective, maintain stability and often longevity of staff. This is helpful to the staff, but more so for the client who needs that consistent social worker. Too often, having to deal with multiple workers over a short period of time is highly stressful. Unfortunately, the ideal conditions are not necessarily the norm. Add to this "resistant" clients or a population that is not happy to have social worker involvement.

There are areas of support services that are better received by clients. But when it comes to child protection, one does not expect to have "satisfied" clients. These are obstacles that have to be overcome. Many amazing social workers, and staff do tremendous work, not because of, but in spite of, the flaws inherent in the system. I also worked alongside many of these very dedicated, caring staff members who did their very best throughout the challenges. I feel very fortunate and privileged to have worked with a great number of children and youth. They taught me valuable lessons every day. They made me a better social worker and person. They showed me that, when tested, the compass works every time.

Limitations of Bureaucracies

As with most government services, it is not a real surprise that it is common to find huge disparities between what the front-line people close to the problem or issue see and experience compared to those further away. Instead of a circular model, where the centre (client) remains in focus from every vantage point, the more common, hierarchical structure leaves no direct, clear view or line to the client. This is not accidental. The front-line workers develop an in-depth understanding of the client and take ownership of the problem. The front-line people are subjected to the demands, expectations, stresses, trauma, disappointments, and blame when the system fails. Sometimes, happiness too, when there is success. The people most "removed" will find it much easier, or at least less painful, when the axe has to come down, as it invariably does.

The cuts often seem arbitrary. They are not based on what works or what doesn't, which service is better than another, what is actually needed, or the best approach of all— prevention. It is well proven that it is best to put resources into prevention since this is the most effective, successful approach. And it actually prevents the need to cut programs since the demand will decrease on its own. It is a matter of putting funds into the programs differently. Prevention rarely gets the priority it needs. Obviously, the model of changing elected officials is a huge part of the problem since no one person "owns" the issue or problem and takes it to a resolution. Depending upon which way the political wind is blowing, there will be "new" programs, "new" studies, a "new" paradigm, "new" strategies. Only to find many were already tried many times before. Regardless, millions of dollars wasted, nothing accomplished, the next year, worst than the last. This is repeated every year, despite comprehensive research, reviews, changes, and improvements agreed upon to make sure "this never happens again" ("tragedy"). But of course, it does, again and again. But new political winds, or appointments, lead to another round of "snakes and ladders." With a set of "new eyes," the process starts again. The financial cost is nothing compared to the cost in human suffering.

It must be said that this is not a local problem. The same issues and problems with how governments operate, their inherent problems, are in fact a global problem. Mass shootings are becoming a daily tragedy in the US with the usual response of how to "make sure this never happens again," but it does every single day and increasingly so. The larger the bureaucracy, the less effective, and accountable, and more wasteful. Some people work tirelessly, others, not so much. There are very few large bureaucracies, if any, that work really well or to the satisfaction of their people. The elected officials and appointees may have been idealistic, well-intentioned people, wanting to bring about some positive change, but soon find themselves suddenly in a clogged system. The longer they remain, the more normalized this becomes, and very little of what they might have hoped for is accomplished. They are no longer "free" agents and must represent the organization. It is not a coincidence that the world's greatest leaders (Gandhi, Nelson Mandala, Martin Luther King, Gloria Steinem, Malala Yousafzai, Greta Thunberg) are never elected officials or politicians. They are free to follow their principles, values, and truths and to speak to them. They have an internal compass, and that is what's most important. Many in the world are outright dictators, tyrants who have zero interest in meeting the needs of their citizens, never mind the planet. These people more frequently appear to become the norm worldwide.

Anyone responsible for program development and evaluating its effectiveness, particularly with taxpayer funds, should refer to books such as Quinn's *Beyond Civilization.* It is truly shocking how little we actually accomplish in addressing chronic, serious problems. Quinn reveals what is wrong with the approach we take. In short, despite programs not being effective or being complete failures, the thinking is that they simply need to be expanded, year after year. Every year we do more of what did not work last year. This is the opposite of evolution, which is based upon devising methods, strategies, and tools to maximize success and sustainability. Once again, humans miss the mark in doing what has occurred in nature for billions of years.

My career taught me that one can care about children, help raise them, and positively impact their lives without giving birth to them. There are many children that need our help in the world.

Things at this stage in my life were generally feeling settled. I had a career I loved. I had structure and routines in my life, time with friends, hobbies, and my beloved dogs. It was, dare I say, almost "uneventful." That was to change in a big way.

IN SEARCH OF A LOST HUMANITY-CULTURAL MUTATION

In 1994, a book, *Ishmael* by Daniel Quinn, began circulating by word of mouth and came to my attention. I decided to read it one weekend. I got comfortable on the couch and began reading *Ishmael.* I lost all track of time and did not go to sleep that night. I read it in one sitting. I could not put it down until I finished it. The effect on me was immediate and powerful. I was no longer the same person I had been just hours before. I also knew I had gained another mentor in Daniel Quinn. However, I had not met him, at least not yet.

Incredulously, I had never heard of Daniel Quinn, so I looked him up. He had published many books, but *Ishmael* won a prestigious award, The Ted Turner Fellowship. It was looking for a fiction book offering creative solutions to global problems. Out of over 2500 entries, *Ishmael* was rightfully determined to be the winner of the half-million-dollar award. Some descriptions of Quinn include "visionary, philosopher, cultural critic, and modern-day prophet."

I soon read others he wrote: *Providence, My Ishmael, The Story of B, Beyond Civilization,* and many more. Much of what I express in this book, particularly in relation to environmental issues and our role on the planet, is rooted in and inspired and influenced by Quinn's writings. I am in no way representing him or any of his written works.

Nothing short of reading Quinn's books directly will capture the power of his words and his wisdom, knowledge, and vast intelligence. The most authentic and accurate depiction of how *Ishmael* and Daniel Quinn impacted me was expressed in a letter I sent him as soon as I finished reading it. Getting a phone call and response directly from Daniel Quinn further validated how genuine he was about making connections with others who shared his message and vision about saving the planet.

Arwinder visiting with Daniel Quinn and wife Rennie in their home in Austin TX.

Clearly, after reading *Ishmael*, I became much more sensitized to the harm we were doing to the planet. Inexplicably, before this moment, I had never rightfully grieved for the suffering and destruction we cause to the planet every single day. I felt extreme sadness and justifiable outrage, but like most other people, it was repressed. I am not embarrassed to admit the overwhelming emotions I felt as hot tears ran uncontrolled down my face. It felt good and right that the floodgates had opened as if a huge bandage had been ripped off my soul, finally exposing my deepest self to feel the pain in a most profound way. That pain I was feeling for the first time was the pain and suffering we were inflicting on every species on the planet. It repulsed me to think of it.

I cried because I grieved for what was being done to the planet: the violence against other animals, the cruelty of destroying their habitat, exterminating them, torturing them by putting them in cages in captivity. I thought of humans putting our worst, most disturbed, violent people in prisons. Worse than that was solitary confinement. Why were we doing this to others on the planet who had committed no crime? Taking babies away from their mothers, for our pathological justification that we were "educating" people by doing this. Or to use them for so-called entertainment and forced labour or greed.

I grieved for animals who were once free that we put in cages, either in our own homes, or in public in zoos and aquariums. I grieved for the life-giving trees that give us oxygen to breathe, without which we would die within seconds. These trees not only fill our lungs, but they also protect us from heavy winds, rain, and the sun.

Their roots keep the soil stable and strong to prevent mudslides. Every single tree provides life and shelter for countless other forms of life, all going about their business without interference. A bird only needs a few twigs to build a nest, lay its eggs, and feed its young. I thought of a bird coming back to that spot to build a nest or feed its young and finding that not only was that tree gone, but all the trees were gone. And everything else with it. This, to the other species, must be like a nuclear bomb going off. Everything destroyed in its community with massive collateral damage. Every single animal, insect, and tree is being subjected to this. Their world is getting smaller literally by the day or minute. How? Why? When had we decided this was acceptable? How was I, and billions of us, going about our daily lives as though things were fine with no shame, no guilt, no sense of urgency about where all this would lead, even for our own existence. I am not a scientist, but I can see that with no oxygen, we die and relatively quickly. With no water, clean water, and access to food, we will die. Most importantly, that the very elements we need to live, to stay alive, are the very things we were happily destroying, eliminating, and exterminating forever.

Human destruction of habitat and torture of all species.

What We Can Learn from Nature

Extinction means there is no return. Billions of diverse species lived as they have always done and allowed us to do the same. They no longer exist for future generations nor for the benefit of biodiversity. Indigenous groups scattered through the planet lived, and are still living, in a balanced, sustainable way. Like all other healthy species, they, too, are being driven to extinction. By force, genocide, and destruction of habitat, their knowledge and way of life is near its end. They, along with all other species, lived on the abundance. There was more than plenty for literally billions of forms of life. Each of them living in various places and ways: in the sky, under the ground, or underwater, and yet, the abundance remained. No matter how many more creatures evolved and were added, everything was proceeding in a stable way. The balance of nature is an incredible phenomenon. No one species was in control of all others. No one was dominant, and each needed something different to survive. Some only ate grass their whole lives. Others ate fish, berries, while others were scavengers preventing waste and disease. Everything produced was of use to others, including so-called waste. If a food source became depleted, the species would adjust, and a balance between its population and available food was maintained. Every species takes the absolute minimum to survive and gives maximum in return. No more. No hoarding, no waste. All this has been going on perfectly well in a complex biosystem for billions of years.

Species thriving in their own habitats.

Destruction of Animals and Denial of Food

Humans are omnivores. We can eat and easily survive on every source of food. But apparently, this is not enough. We want access to every single potential food source and for it to be available all year, any time we want it. If there is a shortage of fish, we do not need to eat fish, but others do. Most species are not omnivores. They usually have limited sources of food, and in some cases, eat only one food source their entire existence, like orca who eat only chinook salmon in the summer.

Some species live on plants or microorganisms not even visible to the human eye. Things we do not even eat. Despite this, we deny them access to it. People think they are "entitled" and have a "right" to eat everything on demand. Even if that means a species starves to death and becomes extinct. These species are contributing to *our* very survival, maintaining the biodiversity of the planet, ensuring air, water, and soil all remain viable and healthy, which, in turn, keeps us alive. We pay them back by denying them food, a habitat, and a chance to raise their young, instead, we pollute their habitat and exterminate them. Why? So, we can construct evermore structures for the sole use of humans. Nothing that puts back into the earth what we take. All other species use the absolute minimum to survive and give the maximum in return. We take more than the maximum and give nothing back. What we "put back" is toxic waste, killing everything on the planet.

Millions are already extinct, and at this rate, most will be in the very near future. This is not just tragic because the mass killing of amazing animals, sea life, and plants, to name a few, leaves the world less beautiful. Though this is true, their existence is required to maintain biodiversity (the immune system) to keep the planet alive, to keep producing oxygen to breathe, water to drink, and viable land for all species. Every one of these species helps keep *us* alive. But each day, we make this less possible because we don't stop ourselves from destroying the planet. This can only be described as being "homicidal and suicidal." At least the "dominant" humans are—the cultural mutants.

What is happening to the parents?

Mothers in nature are fiercely protecting or trying to protect their offspring. We all know the phrase "mama bear," meaning they will fight to their death to protect their young. We have seen images of elephants returning to a place where one died. Many species can be seen grieving the loss of one of their own. These so-called less "intelligent" or less "evolved and primitive" animals show the compassion and empathy that many humans seem to lack.

Some animals, even males, adopt a cross-species offspring. Many animals, even ones considered natural enemies, are creating bonds with each other and loving instead of harming or killing. Even if they suffered terrible conditions and violence, they manage to regain trust and give love. This is incredible. Animals are becoming more compassionate and "humane" while many of us are not.

In contrast with humans, an image of a species creating bonds and nurturing across species.

One species, humans, continues to destroy the earth. It has been a life-giving and sustaining paradise. We are turning it into hell for us and all others on the planet. It makes no sense. I felt outraged and wanted to run out and shout, "Wake up, everyone. What are we doing? How come we are talking about our vacations, and people are shopping away, getting their hair done, nails polished, and watching their 'reality shows,' and acting like everything is 'normal' and carrying on with life as it is?"

Contrast from nature's beauty to what is created by humans.

Shockingly, how could billions of people who have children claim to love their children and be fine with what we are all doing to the planet? Granted, there are individuals, families, parents, children, and groups trying to do their best to lighten the so-called human footprint. But why is this even a "choice?" Why is it up to an individual to "choose" if they want to live without harming the planet? Why should someone be able to "choose" producing or buying harmful products rather than "green" ones? Why should "green" items be more expensive than ones that are harmful? People would prefer to buy everything that is not harmful to their children and the planet, and no one should be put in a position where they must choose the harmful one. People can't just go out and intentionally poison their neighbour. They'd go to prison for that. So why should this be any different? It needs to be illegal and criminal to sell anything on the planet for consumption or use when there are perfectly safe alternatives available. If they were the only ones available, they would cost less, and not put people in the impossible position of choosing "less expensive but more harmful."

Some people might be tempted to assume people like me, and others who chose to be childless, think, "Why should I care?" Ironically, too many with children do not seem to have the sense of urgency one would expect, considering the accelerating destruction of the earth. Yes, that includes billions of humans—your children, the children of so-called "pro family" politicians, religious leaders, teachers, lawyers, judges, professors, students, doctors, labourers, CEOs, and homemakers. Every one of these groups has children and grandchildren but continue consuming, poisoning, destroying, and killing all life on the planet that their children are supposed to inherit.

The Harmful Effects of Consumerism

Everyone's shopping, buying multiple items so everyone can have the same items in every room of the house—evidence of our pathological, obsessive desire to consume and hoard. Serious hoarding is considered a mental health condition. In the Diagnostic and Statistical Manual of Mental Disorders (DSM-5), hoarding disorder is described as a "persistent difficulty discarding or parting with possessions regardless of their actual value." It is a potential sign of anxiety or depression. Is this what is ailing billions of us? People hoard animals that have to be seized by animal rescue organizations. People hoard children that have to be removed by child protection organizations. We take animals and children away from these individuals because, even though they hoard, they don't actually love them or care for them. In fact, these animals and children are subjected to starvation and horrendous pain and suffering. How do we deal with this on such a mass level when billions of us are doing this? How do we prevent ourselves from hoarding the planet? It seems it could very well be a sign of our "sickness." During Covid-19, the hoarding left the supermarket shelves empty, and some stores put restrictions on items and hired security to prevent hostilities from breaking out. This was not as a result of accessing water or food but items to stock.

Hoarding.

The mutant culture devours every item and species on the planet. No other species on the planet is taking or consuming anything we require to survive. Nor are any of them overpopulating the planet and causing any shortage of land, water, food, or living space for humans. None are denying humans anything.

<u>Overpopulation</u>

Humans, conversely, continue to overpopulate the planet, the surface which consists mostly of water. The actual available landmass is getting smaller by the day. As the water table continues to rise (land at sea level will be submerged), this will result in an extreme shortage of land for almost eight billion of us here now. Our current population is not survivable or sustainable. But we have not stopped or decreased the number of human babies being born. In fact, there are almost 400,000 (**four hundred thousand**) babies born in the world *every single day.*

A small planet with little land mass unsustainable for ever increasing human population.

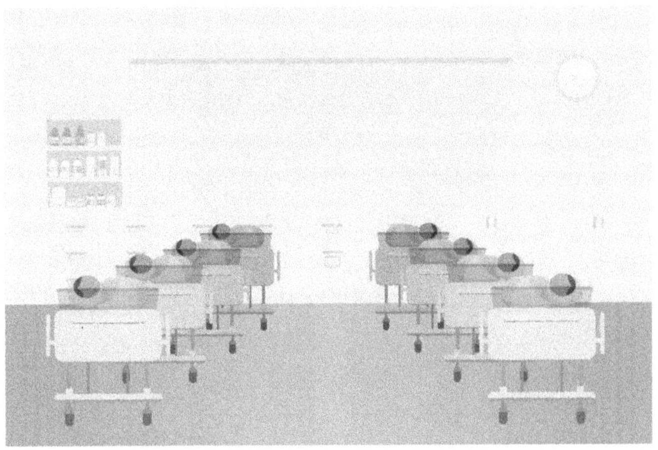

Like a Cancer-The Mutant Culture

Here's an analogy, albeit disturbing: We are behaving in a manner that resembles cancer cells. We invade an area on the planet, keep replicating rapidly like cancer cells until cancer ultimately takes over its healthy host. But it cannot stop itself, so rather than allowing the host to stay alive and live longer, it, too, dies by killing its host. This is what we are doing: overpopulating the planet and killing all the healthy cells (plants, trees, insects, birds, sea life, large mammals, and all life that makes up biodiversity) until the host is weakened and too fragile to survive—the constant, overwhelming assault on all its systems, causing death. For decades, we have been warned this will be the result, but we just keep on killing and destroying, and in the process, kill ourselves. Like a terminally ill person is told, "One more cigarette will kill you," we just keep puffing away. Cancer cells don't respond to fear. They just boldly charge ahead until it all comes to an end.

What is going on? What "system" have we created? Why are we so out of control? Isn't this what a cancer cell is? A mutation of a healthy gene that becomes a cancerous one. All the other species are the "healthy" genes, including Indigenous groups. We are the only ones mutated into destructive ones. The healthy cells we kill off, making them extinct. We allow the unhealthy mutated gene to replicate at an alarming rate (400,000 a day and increasing). The host, Earth, is in critical condition and on life support. If we want to survive, we must cure ourselves of this cultural mutation. The stomping out of diverse populations of animal and plant life is weakening our "immune" system. Our bodies require healthy, numerous white blood cells to attack and fight against infection and disease. Biodiversity is ours, the Earth's "white blood cells." If something enters the ecosystem, all the healthy species work together to rid the threat and keep the planet healthy and in balance. No one species can come in and threaten the whole because there are too many layers of protection to allow this to happen. One species or its population may decrease to maintain the balance, but the diverse immune system of the planet will protect the whole.

But one species designated itself dominant on the planet. The mutant one. Humans are not superior. We are destructive and lethal in terms of how we live. We don't protect human life or the planet. We cannot survive as a single species, a mutant species. More of us are beginning to understand the importance of having billions (too late for this since many are extinct) of diverse animals, plants, and life forms to maintain the health of the planet. This system was, and is, already in place. Every day we are learning the mistakes of our past: clear-cutting, cutting down the Amazon (literally our lungs), diverting water systems or obstructing them, building damns and seawalls, and building on steep hills or cliffs where our actions have destabilized the integrity of the soil, leading to massive mudslides. Climate change (the watered-down phrase from global warming, as this was too alarming) is causing the melting of snow caps, killing all life there, and raising the water table, which will submerge land at sea level. Planners are frantically looking at ways to repair this, but more importantly, realizing that the ecosystem has already provided us with the blueprints. Anything we create or build should adapt to and work in concert with nature's blueprint. This blueprint is being followed successfully by every living thing on the planet for billions of years with total success until we decided our blueprint was better. We would just override and overpower, use lethal force, to make nature submit and adapt to us. We are now seeing the devastating, destructive consequences of disregarding nature's blueprint—record numbers of hurricanes, floods, and fires. We are a planet in chaos, desperately trying to find that balance that has been in place for billions of years. If we could have paced ourselves to adapt to nature's blueprint, we could have averted all this. But regardless of scientific and observable evidence, we keep on full speed ahead. How can the so-called most intelligent species on the planet not get what billons of others have? How can we instead behave as a cancer cell?

Increased violent weather systems like Hurricanes, Tsunamis, Fires and Floods.

Are We Pathological?

Forensic psychologists and experts have studied the most disturbed criminals, ones that have committed sadistic crimes. They have similar traits in their backgrounds. Animal cruelty is often a key marker; it represents the worse potential for violence in adulthood. It serves as a red flag that something is deeply wrong. What does that tell us about our species? About the mutant culture? We don't think about ourselves this way. But it's time that we do. We need to see how we treat animals, whether in the wild, in captivity, as pets in cages, for entertainment or harsh labour, poaching (for ivory), or using them for experiments. This is and should be seen as pathological and disturbed. We need to stop normalizing it. We are no longer horrified at what we see or do. This is animal cruelty and sadistic in the worse possible way. We consider violent criminals in desperate need of incarceration, generally incorrigible and in need of counselling, treatment, and healing. As a species, we desperately need help. We seem to be in a vicious cycle. The more we destroy the planet, the more pathological we become. No other species behaves as we do. They are not suffering the plight of humans. The self-created suffering, emotionally and psychologically. Indigenous groups who live by respecting the earth live in a balanced way; they did not suffer our pathologies. Why? Because they observe and follow nature's blueprint. Previous generations lived sustainably without killing themselves and the planet and it can be achieved again. Fortunately, we have access to nature's blueprint too. We know what it is, and we need to follow it. We need to turn back to nature. Powerful yet gentle. Patient, benevolent, equal, fair. No one species is treated better than another. All have equal access to live in a healthy, balanced way: no cruelty, no captivity, no suffering, no torture, no one hunting them to extinction or destroying their habitat. We have to get along like the rest of the inhabitants on the planet.

The gentle yet powerful force of nature reclaiming space for itself and its beauty.

Its not just our hostility to other species. Humans have a "zillion" reasons why we can't get along with each other. Humans are literally enemies, destroying each other for money or resources. Wars, gangs, mafia, drug lords, dealers, criminal enterprises, trafficking in humans, including children (for labour and sex slaves), and animals.

Collage of suffering created and inflicted upon our own species.

The world is full of random violence, thrill kills, copycat kills, killing for fame, mass killing, and school shootings. People are hurt, bullied, abused, killed, abducted, and held hostage for money. Everywhere is police brutality, conflicts, violent overthrows of tyrannical leaders, and conflicts based on racism, sexism, religion, sexual orientation, and class. We have entire departments dedicated to prenatal harm, child abuse, childhood trauma, sexual assault, rape, abuse by the church, senior abuse, elderly abuse, abuse of vulnerable disabled people, domestic abuse, and pet abuse. We have discrimination, harassment, and bullying at the workplace. Just about everyone qualifies for some source of PTSD.

No other species is subjecting us to this. No other species subjects their own species or offspring to this.

Instances where this may occur in other species (killing their own or abandoning a weaker member) are related to ensuring the success of itself as a group, not due to a pathology, as our behaviour is. Unlike in these animals, it does not lead to our survival. This is a uniquely human-on-human phenomenon. Totally self-inflicted.

WHAT OF THE CHILDREN?

As a social worker for almost thirty years, I saw firsthand the damage caused to children in the immediate and the community and society long term. The effects rarely remained contained to an individual or family, and often, the cycle of abuse, neglect, and being in government care becomes multigenerational. I was a social worker to children who aged out as adults and had children that I then became the social worker for with the next generation. Unfortunately, the issues that become chronic in society become normalized, and we react to the crisis, rarely addressing or resolving the root causes. The parents whose children come into government care are varied and have a multitude of complex histories and issues. Increasingly, addiction and substance misuse by parents and caregivers results in serious neglect and harm to the infant or child(ren).

If someone is abusing children, the abuser has to be dealt with immediately. Stop the abuse. Remove the abuser, preventing them from having access to the child, any child, and stop the suffering. Instead, the child is removed and placed into an alternate home, which causes additional trauma and harm to the child. But the process requires numerous steps to allow the parents an opportunity to overcome their challenges for the possibility of the child returning to their care. This process often takes a number of years. Now the child may have begun to bond with the alternate caregiver, only to be placed back with the parents if deemed safe. This causes another severing of an attachment. The child may no longer feel as attached to the biological parents anymore. They may begin to show signs of distress by acting up.

The child may be traumatized for decades (in and out of care), and often siblings also come into care. Hopefully, they would be placed together but depending on the number of siblings and "beds" available, this may not be possible. If the child received protection quickly and had a stable long-term placement in a healthy home, they could fare better. But the stressed systems are rarely able to provide ideal conditions for the child, and sometimes it may be a worse situation than what they had with their own parents. So often, the cycle of abuse and neglect continues, which negatively impacts society, and an increased need for services remains inadequate.

But for some communities, particularly those of Indigenous families, services may be almost non-existent. Addiction and suicide remain epidemic. The communities may be isolated and very impoverished. These communities also suffer from multigenerational struggles because of the devastation of their culture when the Europeans took over the entire Indigenous peoples, including violently exterminating them. They abducted by force all the children and placed them in residential schools. Here they received every form of abuse possible by so-called religious people. At the time of this writing in Kamloops BC, 215 remains of children have been unearthed from a site of a past residential school. This is likely the tip of the iceberg and finally proves what the Indigenous families have been claiming happened to the missing children. It's no surprise that Indigenous people are distrusting of services or support by agencies or those in authority. The devastation of a close-knit, proud people mean they are still struggling to find their way back from the hell that became their life through no doing of their own. How does anyone, an entire culture, recover from that? Also introduced, with devastating effects, was smallpox (and other diseases) and alcohol. How are Indigenous people able to raise healthy children when they lost their culture, identity, language, attachments, role models, and way of life, including their sacred connection to the land, animals, the planet? This is how the cycle of abuse and neglect has been repeated for generations. They are slowly finding their way back, and governments and society are learning that what was done to the Indigenous people was an atrocity, and amends and restitution must be made. Many of us are rooting for them to regain what they lost (though, of course, that is impossible). We need them right now to teach us what we also lost. Rather than following their way of life, it was stomped out and replaced with the mutated culture—a destructive culture. Now the time has come to accept the Indigenous way of life as the healthy, sustainable way to live on the planet and save ourselves and the planet from total collapse. We are fortunate the Indigenous people are still with us and gaining strength, their voice, and support in this path back to living without destroying the earth. In their way of life, raising children was a shared responsibility. The child was the centre of the tribe, and all would ensure their safety and well-being. It was a very safe and secure way for a child to live within the tight-knit community. Raising healthy children was everyone's business and necessary to maintain the success and stability of the tribe. They did all this without anything from outside the tribe. No government, no program, no services. They and many other tribes and cultures even practiced (and still do) rituals using plants or substances such as hallucinogens. They have visions that are considered spiritual and linked to the sacred world, the earth. No one became addicted or committed crimes or harmed others to get more. It was valued but not misused or allowed to take over their lives or their responsibilities to their children or the tribe, except in one culture.

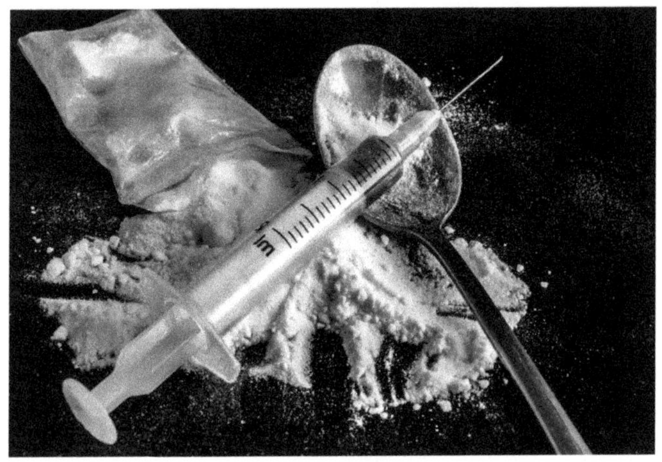

Devastation from drug misuse.

To Have or Not—Biology or Messaging?

Is it a fact that men and women have a natural, inborn desire to have children? I know many who never had this. I never had this. How can we conclude having children results from pure biology without acknowledging many girls are culturally programmed for assuming this role or goal? Would corporations spend billions every year encouraging marriage and convincing people to have children if they could rely on biology to simply dictate this? We know marketing dollars are spent because they work.

The Australian Bureau of Statistics says that sometime in the next decade, the number of couples without children will overtake the number of couples with.

Research shows women's reasons for choosing not to have children are multifaceted and complex. Overpopulation and climate change, a lacking maternal instinct, health concerns and a desire for independence and freedom are just a few. Many are concerned about the state of the planet and a concern about the perilous future they are leaving behind to a child.

I am challenging this view that universally there is an inborn desire to procreate. If there was, contraceptives would not have been sought and used. Also, humans don't make all choices based on biology. We have free choice and intention and plan for the future in a way that animals don't. Just as men are biologically stronger than women do not mean they should use their strength to control women, though Neanderthals may have done so. We do not find this acceptable. There is a strong desire and drive for sex. That ends up producing offspring, children, whether desired or not. Desire of sex does not equal desire for children. Ask a teenager if he wants sex or to be a father. The procreation drive, if true, should be followed by a drive to nurture and care, and we know this is not the case in humans as it is in animals.

In many cultures, millions of children are born around the world because women do not have control of their bodies or reproductive freedom. How many would delay, have fewer or no children if we had true reproductive freedom? Currently, in the US, terminating a pregnancy, even in a case of rape or incest, has become criminalized. This is the most oppressive assault on a woman's right to chose in the US since Roe vs Wade was enacted (and under threat at this moment by the so-called public servants). In other places in the world, even a miscarriage can result in charges and imprisonment for the female if authorities suspect that it was a termination. If women have the innate, inborn desire to procreate, why is there a historic increase in forcing women to have children? This is a question that needs to be considered. Corporations and politicians definitely want to promote population increase. They know they can't just rely on biology.

Since the Village Pays, Should it Not have a Say?

In the mutant culture, people often have the view that they can raise their children however they want and can have as many children as they want. Not taking into account the overpopulation issue, what is the cost to society and the planet when parents raise abused, violent individuals who inflict pain on the rest of us? Is this a "right?" Don't others have a "right" to be safe? Should not society (the village) have an interest in the health of their community? Is our emphasis on "privacy" and "individualism" (wants, not needs) a justifiable reason to continue creating an ever-growing, violent society? Is it not healthier for the child and society when everyone takes an interest in raising healthy children? Is this not a better model which provides layers of safety nets for the child? For all the children? If something happens to a parent, or even both parents, in tribalistic cultures, there is no disruption to the child. No severing of ties and loss of the family and community sense of belonging. Is this not more sustainable because no one needs taxpayer or government services to care for the child? No waitlists on an overburdened system, which often does more harm than good. This child will not have psychological scars from being neglected and repeatedly traumatized from changing homes and losing family ties. Why this works is because tribalistic cultures don't view children as possessions. The parent does not own them. They belong to the tribe. But the mutant culture looks at everything in terms of ownership—our trees, our ocean, our children. This approach is causing the destruction of a sense of belonging and a sense of security and identity. Conversely, in tribes, if both parents die, the child still has their tribe, their sense of belonging and identity. It never gets lost.

The mutant culture wants others not to care, to "mind their own business," because these children are "mine." They don't belong to you. You have no say or interest, and if I can't look after them, well, such is life. Either the child will not be well cared for, or the government will have to get involved and take over the parenting. A tribe does not leave the important role of raising children on the shoulders of two parents or, as in the mutant culture, often a single parent with no extended family or generations living together that can help. In a tribe, no one person is burdened, as the tribe has a built-in support system for life and at no cost. Should people raise children in this way? Is the mutant culture working for the parent, the child, or society? I say no, it is not. Look at what the child and society lose when we raise children as possessions. Society suffers when children are not given a chance for a healthy, safe, secure upbringing.

Child shackled ball and chain.

According to the World Health Organization "Half of the world's children, or approximately **1 billion children each year** are affected by physical, sexual, or psychological violence, suffering injuries, disabilities, and death, because countries have failed to follow established strategies to protect them".

<u>Financial Cost to the village.</u>

In terms of costs related to assuming care for infants and children who were prenatally exposed to harmful substances or who are abused or neglected the costs are exorbitant and increasing every year. This is not sustainable, and the services fall short of needs year after year.

Increases in hospital costs and subsequent child welfare programs for parents usually focus on sobriety. Repeat cycles of relapses increase trauma for a child. Potential lifelong challenges include foster homes or specialized residential services; speech behaviour therapy; cognitive, intellectual, medical, and physical disabilities; outreach services; specialized educational assistance and programs; behavioural challenges; difficulties with trust and relationships; at risk for running away, substance use, and pathways to delinquency and adult systems.

These incidents and the costs of babies born addicted go up year after year. Addiction issues are becoming the primary cause of child welfare involvement. No real prevention programs are proactively aimed at reducing the incidence of prenatal exposure. Most only come into play during pregnancy and post-birth. This is too late. This does not reduce the numbers born or the need for services.

Women are supposed to be treated with respect and empowered. I agree. Does the current approach actually do this for women? I believe there is another perspective that seems taboo to discuss, as so many issues are in the mutant culture. As a woman, I would feel insulted if I were a pregnant woman suffering with addiction. Baby after baby is removed; there is never a message that I am capable of making less harmful choices. No one suggests there is. No one expects me to. They expect me to just keep doing what I am doing. Keep going to the same programs that don't work. We know that for many women, and anyone for that matter, staying clean and sober successfully, long term, is near impossible. If it were easy, rich and famous celebrities, with everything at their fingertips, would not be repeatedly relapsing and dying from overdose in record numbers every year. Do we really expect or believe these parents can overcome addiction? We know they can't, except for the smallest percentage of them.

If it were easy, surely parents, women, who have had one, two, three, and up to twelve children removed and placed in government care could stop for the sake of their babies? That is the ultimate deterrent, no? No, it is not as we have seen with the low success rate of staying clean and sober. But they are set up for failure. They go through having a child removed, the court process, and mandated counselling services. The cycle is, after a person is initially clean and sober, they go through a very positive phase where they truly believe that this time, for sure, they will be able to maintain sobriety. Anyone who has gone through this with a loved one will attest that the addict's conviction is genuine and totally convincing. So next time, for sure, a healthy baby will be possible. A relapse happens, and now they are back to the beginning of the cycle. And on and on it goes as the tragic number of babies born addicted rises. This leads the woman to further feelings of failure, guilt, remorse, shame, isolation, and relapse. How does this help a woman feel empowered? It does NOT. It makes her feel powerless to do differently or to make any other choices since other choices are not discussed. So, the message is, "We know you can't stop this. We know it can't be prevented, so we all continue letting the tragic process play out time after time." No one expects different, and no one says different. But the only part she can't stop is the addiction part. She can prevent the doing harm to a baby part.

But we can't "force" a woman. It is her body. Of course not, but the baby is born in a society (village), and this baby, once no longer in the womb, now becomes part of society. A society incapable of preventing the suffering too and cannot provide adequate services or resources with the unsustainable cost of even one single baby born addicted.

Remember, these are not babies born from the already increasing, negative impact of environmental toxins in the air that we ingest daily. Or due to genetic or other reasons. I am only speaking here about the ones that are 100 percent preventable. The ones that are the most prevalent, harmful, and costly are preventable. Isn't this actually *good* news? We can't talk about this issue. Can't consider some options to stop this cycle because we don't want to offend anyone? Really? This is the reason society seems locked into a system that grows its problems and costs exponentially because no one dares state the obvious or comes up with any potential solutions. We just sit back and watch, observe as bystanders. Oh well, too bad no one can do anything. We just have to have more people suffer, have less money every year to pay for all the things we need for our families, for our health and education—forget about the planet. Well, I am not an elected official, so I am not concerned about maintaining my job in office (who never seems to actually get the work done). I am not a politician who has to be "politically correct." I am simply a person with a compass.

Are we beginning the conversation of prevention early enough? Many people develop substance misuse very young, often by high school. Is this whole area of prenatal risk to baby if substances are used during pregnancy discussed? Have young people had a chance to truly understand how their life, and that of the infant, will often result in the need for life-long services. Have they considered the cost to society? What of the chances of relapses resulting in future incidents of prenatal exposure? Do they get an opportunity to see firsthand (as part of this education) what the baby endures and how young moms cope with parenting a substance-exposed baby? The stresses on her and her social, educational goals? What could a young woman do to prevent this before she became pregnant by choice or not? Include young men in this education as well. They, too, play a role in prevention. Could an effective program in high school play a part in the goal of prevention?

Failing this educational work, what about connecting with a woman (and her partner) at the first instance of a pregnancy where addiction is diagnosed to be a problem? Aside from offering prenatal services to promote the health of baby and mom and reduce harm during this pregnancy, what discussion is there for after the baby's birth? Everyone wants the mom to achieve sobriety, and even though we know the statistics, and the mom knows as well, it will be difficult, maybe unlikely. But we play this out as though it will be likely. Instead of focusing on abstinence or "harm reduction" (relating to the nature and frequency of the substance use, as is the norm), how about having a more spiritual perspective, a biological, eco-psychological perspective of a mother's powerful instinct and desire to protect her offspring from harm? Like all other species have. The harm to the current baby was not prevented, but how about going forward? Not with the typical approach of telling or encouraging her not to use during pregnancy. Realistically, very few people are not aware of this message.

A more spiritual, realistic approach could be taken with mom (and partner), fully engaged at the point of first contact—an acknowledgement that addiction struggles are insidious with a disclosure that the success rate of all programs is low. It's not a failure on the addict's part but the nature of the disease. That the need to use, when it comes during pregnancy has an equally harmful effect on the mother in the sense that, innately, a mother's instinct is to protect her offspring, cause them no harm. But with addiction, this is a near-impossible goal regardless of how much they want to reach it. How is her trauma exacerbated once she gives birth to an addicted baby? Will the added stress, shame, and guilt, trigger more substance use? If staying clean and sober is near impossible, how might she be able to prevent harm to another baby? (We know in society women are pressured to want a baby and have a baby.) Harm reduction does not only apply to substance use. Is the ultimate harm reduction not preventing more prenatal exposure? If she has had one baby but gets sufficient support at this junction to maintain the connection bond with the baby, with intense support in caring for that baby, it has the potential to prevent the trauma of losing care of the baby. Hopefully, she will have a more positive attachment to the baby, not severing the bond, which surely triggers many to use, numb the pain, and experience more trauma. Better to feel some success in being a capable mother, despite her addiction. How many women have a subsequent baby to fill the need, the void, after the first one has been removed from her care, for years, permanently? We have already touched upon the issue that even if there is a biological desire for a child, this does not translate into caring for them.

During this spiritual, therapeutic relationship, can there be a totally honest and realistic in-depth discussion, free from judgement, about what option she feels she could be most successful at? Could she remain clean and sober (substance free) or pregnancy free? Nothing would be forced in this regard. It is simply a self-analysis process she is asked to undertake. There will be no judgement about admitting that she will use or does not want to stop using. There are many people who have no intention or desire to quit using, but they are not going to vocalize this. So, they play the role others expect.

The mother decides what she believes would be achievable and the better option for her. Take the stigma away from insisting that she must be able to stay clean and sober in order to keep the baby she has had. But going forward, what is the best plan to ensure the optimum harm reduction for herself and the ultimate harm reduction for her offspring? Maybe this is being able to parent one baby or child, with extensive supports, while using. Is this approach not actually empowering the woman? Accept that she may not be able to stop using, but she can prevent further harm.

Now, everyone behaves as it is "business as usual." Just keep everything as is, with no one making any progress on a totally preventable issue that is impacting millions of babies and children every year and impacting society's lack of resources while radically increasing the financial burden, not to mention life-long struggles for the affected children. Is this approach not worth a try since we don't seem to have any prevention plan in place, at least none that actually work?

When it comes to issues relating to the planet, we dismiss them. When it comes to issues relating to humans, we ignore them. Every year we behave as though everything is the way it is, it will get worse every year, and there is not one thing we can do about it. I disagree. I think we need to stop treating humans as helpless, hopeless victims who simply cannot do anything to stop doing what they do. They can make better choices. We have not been presenting them in a way that treats them as capable, willing people who want to do something to improve their life and situation, despite having a substance-use problem. This spiritual approach empowers and respects and allows some hope of doing something positive, having some success in their life. They may not have been able to stop using, but they helped protect a baby from harm. What could be more heroic than that? And further, they made a significant, positive impact on reducing the stress and burden on systems that cannot care for even the healthy individuals in society. That outcome seems more probable to me, worth a new look and a new approach. It is something the woman can feel good about. Positive about. She is not worthless and helpless. She is powerful enough to save and protect a baby from lifelong harm because she can prevent it. Wow. A whole different perspective.

Is it a privilege to have a child or a right? It is clear that biologically having a child in no way qualifies the person to be a good parent. How do we, as a society, find ways to balance competing needs or wants or entitlements that we assumed to be rights? Making sure babies and children are fed, free from neglect and abuse, continues to elude the mutant culture. With all kinds of programs, services, interventionists, paediatricians, mental health experts, and parenting experts, we can't make sure babies and children are properly care for? Why, when we have thousands of law enforcement officers, policy and lawmakers, lawyers, judges, justice department people, and counsellors? In fact, we are doing the worst job on the planet, as can be seen by the reports cited above. Is this the sign of a healthy society able to raise a healthy community? Are these not the signs of humanity in distress? Are these not the red flags that need our immediate attention? Not just from an agency. No child welfare system seems to or really can do an adequate job. They can't protect every single child. North America certainly does not, and the US is particularly problematic, with the additional risk of violence and death of children due to guns. In order for child abuse and neglect to be happening, there are too many people looking the other way, putting their own wants over the needs of their children and not doing the right thing. Where is the "compass" for millions, billions of us?

What is the remedy to keep society safe and prevent this cycle? Why does the so-called dominant species not know how to do the most critical and important thing all life is based on? Why does having and raising healthy offspring not come very naturally to far too many of us? Even with all the books, experts, free access to information, and hands-on support, many struggles to raise truly healthy children. Was this not the most powerful natural instinct?

Violence Born from Suffering

Many humans have been the victim of violence and have felt powerless and vulnerable. Sometimes people try to reclaim their power by inflicting violence on others in the same manner that they were violated. But our pain, real or perceived, is no justification for abusing animals or people. If this is the case, that means it's open season for billions of us. Almost everyone has a story. There are people who have had a charmed life but feel they were cheated out of something. In these times of Covid, some people are comparing the recommendation or mandate to wear a mask to the Holocaust! Is this real suffering? Billions are struggling. Does that mean we can expect and accept people inflicting pain on us?

We hear this in the court systems all the time: The person suffered in their childhood. That may very well be true and horrible. But this is not a reason or rationale to subject others to even worse pain and suffering. Why are we harming our own species? We seem to accept everything without ever changing the conditions creating these ills in society. Contrary to nature, our adaptability is leading to our destruction and of the planet. We have continued to "adapt" to or accept a lowering of our quality of life in every facet of life. Where are the principles, values, and boundaries that should be helping us do that right thing? They are absent, lacking, or ignored.

Humans have created and inflicted conditions for suffering, such as starvation, poverty, disease, and lack of clean water or shelter. This is a result of human actions, such as overpopulation and denial of fair, equal access to the Earth's life-giving ecosystem. Ironically, species, even those we refer to as savage or deadly, literally starving and threatened, are not killing us. People who are starving for food and water are not directly killing us. They just want food and water. They may kill each other, but this is not because the Earth does not have air, water, shelter, or food, but because of those who want to control it and deny it to others for profit. I met many destitute and starving people in India. There are many around the world today. None committed violence against me for food, water, or anything. One might consider it justified if they did so. But that is not usually the source of the violence. Why is the self-appointed ruler of the universe the most "fragile" and emotionally and psychologically unable to cope? Record numbers die from suicide every year. Dying from drug overdose is an epidemic. Not because of our "struggle" to survive. We have air, water, and food. Unless, of course, we include suffering created around the world. How does Nature operate?

THE ART AND SCIENCE OF NATURE

The successful, pre-existing eco-strategies in nature should make life much easier for us. We created the problems and crises on the planet but do not need to invent all the solutions. We need to adopt the existing strategies, successful for billions of years. We need to do what was already being done. As humans, all our creations and inventions originate from observing, and in fact, replicating the natural world. It is doubtful we would have known how to design a plane if we did not observe how birds fly. Would we even have conceived flight was possible had we not watched a bird fly? We would not have known that we needed flippers or how to design them to enable us to swim underwater had we not observed aquatic and sea life. The observation of the intricate, beautiful geometric design of a spider web helped us understand engineering. Geometry is considered complex math for humans. We did not "create it." We did see it. There is very little in our lives that does not have its origins and roots in nature. We have allowed ourselves and our children to forget this.

From the moment we wake up to when we go to sleep, we are living and surviving on only what the Earth provides. We breathe the air (even while we sleep), have our coffee or beverage, eat breakfast, drink water throughout the day, eat fruits, meats, dairy, fish, vegetables, use honey, or whatever. Some will have wine, beer, or juice with dinner. Every one of these we get from nature, the Earth, as does every other living thing on the planet. Not one species survives on anything that does not come from the Earth.

Every one of us is dependent on the planet to live each day. Nature is not just there to be consumed by humans—a passive, inert, "object" without purpose. Nature has a system, a blueprint, in place to sustain all life on the planet. This blueprint **must** be followed by every species, including us, to survive.

Frankly, this is comforting because that helps us solve the critical threat, we all face. We don't have to flounder around, looking, seeking, scratching our heads, being hopeless or helpless. Nature, as always, "has our back." The solutions are already in place for us to see and follow. That is amazing and fortunate for the human race and the future of the planet.

Humans have misplaced ideas about our superior position on the planet, that other species know nothing and are "simple and unintelligent." But as mentioned above, there is little that we have not learned from nature. All our intelligence and "inventions" are rooted in nature. It has been going on since the beginning of time and has continued to evolve in increasingly complex ways to ensure maximum potential for survival by a maximum number of species.

Scientists, such as Marcus du Sautoy (mathematician and author), are continuing to discover that every living species on the planet is operating on a mathematical code that contains the rules that govern everything on the planet and the universe. That certain insects only emerge from underground, in a graduated schedule. Some emerge in thirteen-year cycles, while others on a different cycle. This maximizes the survival of each species; otherwise, they would be subject to starvation if they all emerged and needed resources at the same time. At the time this writing in fact such an event occurred with the emergence of the cicada after their 17-year cycle. They will appear again in 17 years. Life on the planet is working in connection and in concert together. Without that, biodiversity, vital to survival, could not occur or exist. Nature's "geometric code" is referred to as "fractal." It is defined as "a pattern that the laws of nature repeat at different scales."

Symmetry: A Journey into the Patterns of Nature Paperback – Illustrated, March 3, 2009

by Marcus du Sautoy (Author)

There is also a BBC documentary called The Code which features Marcus du Sautoy where he discusses this in great detail and with real life examples. He has found that in some of the patterns and cycles followed by insects for example, that prime numbers are preferred for their cycles.

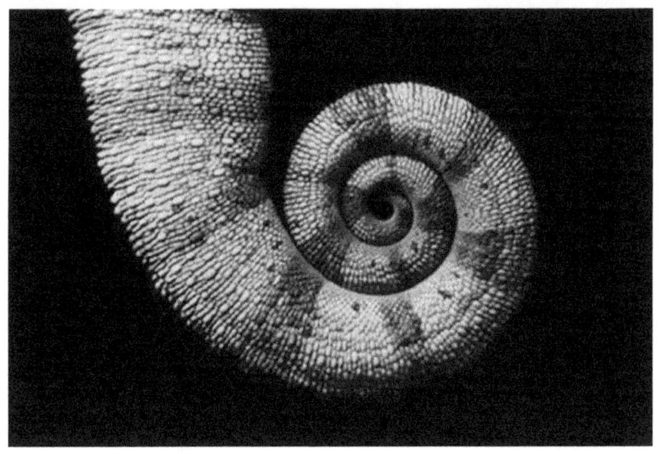

Examples of Fractals present in every species in nature.

Fractals are not only geometric but incredibly beautiful—science and art in nature. Humans need to start understanding and following nature's blueprint instead of destroying nature and forever losing the knowledge, our way, and survival. This blueprint should be exciting and comforting because we don't have to create the solution. We need to implement it in everything we do, from big and small. We have to get beyond thinking and living in a way that is contrary to the survival of the planet. Nature has given us the way.

Look at anything in nature, and one can easily see these fractals (patterns). The symmetry is evident in flowers, plants, trees, shells (such as a nautilus), vegetables, coastlines, ocean waves, spider webs, insects, animals, and infinitely more.

These patterns and mathematical cycles and formulas are present everywhere. Every bit of nature is powerfully expressing its intelligence, science, and beauty. Each flower, insect, and animal share the same geometric codes of life. We did not create any of them. Our arrogance and concept of superiority have been our undoing and is a delusion on our part. We are barely skilled as observers, beyond what has been obvious. It is only recently becoming apparent that humans understand the least how nature works and what is required to live sustainably and successfully. All other species have managed to do it successfully without any formal education or human input. We refuse to be humbled by the absolute brilliance and ultimate benevolence of nature. Why are we attempting to compete with scientific intelligence, pre-existing our appearance on the planet by billions of years? We only need to follow nature's blueprint for the survival of the planet.

Some of what nature and biodiversity contributes or provides for our survival and life:

Fresh water, pollination, seed dispersal, pest control, health, medicine, fisheries, biodiversity and wildlife abundance, climate regulation, economy, art.

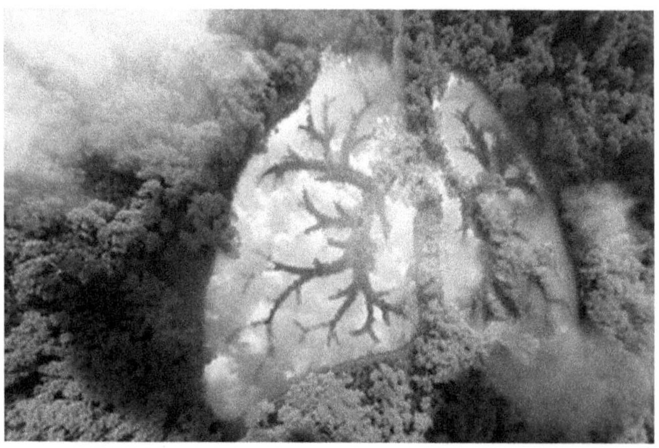

Producers of oxygen for our "lungs" and the planets.

<u>Nature Doesn't Need Us</u>

The planet, and certainly none of the species, need humans to survive. They did extremely well before our arrival and will do so if or when we no longer remain. In fact, they will do better without us. We need to understand it is humans that need other species to survive. It is their presence and contribution to biodiversity and the elements that allow us to survive. Their existence gives us the air to breathe, water to sustain life, soil to provide nutrients, and roots that provide stability to the ground and trees. Our ecosystem provides the bees and insects that pollinate the plants and flowers we need to give us food like honey from their hard work. Nothing is insignificant on the planet. It would not have remained if it were. The sun, the moon, clouds, lightning, all play a vital part in the life and survival of the planet. We created none of these. They are not *ours*—don't "belong" to us. Nothing in the natural world is or should be treated as "our" commodity to sell, use, destroy or deny to others. Billions of other life forms need the same things to survive. They took care of the elements so that we, too, could live. They did not destroy, pollute or prevent us from having access to any of it. They took the bare minimum to sustain life and no more. We are hoarding, polluting, and destroying it, denying it to the other species. What kind of sociopaths are we? This is extremely disturbing behaviour. We seem to have an abusive relationship with the natural world. To us, other species or nature appears passive, not a "threat," so we think we can "bully" or take advantage of them, which we do.

Local images taken by Arwinder of raccoon and mom duck and ducklings trying to live and raise their young in our mutant world.

For most of us, since we live in congested cities with a dense human population, we barely notice nature. We have to go to designated places like parks or go "out of the city" to see it, be with it. In the parks and areas near us, nature tends to make gentle sounds, but we drown it out with our noises. But in nature, most animals need to be quiet and still for their survival. Walk into a trail, and you have to really search to find anything. They don't all come out, swarm us, confront us, attack us, or drive us away. The only reason one might be "aggressive" is to protect their young. They are supposed to do this. Or another reason could be that they are dying of starvation, usually because of our actions, causing their loss of habitat or source of food. The last thing any other species wants is to come into contact with the most dangerous, invasive species on the planet: *us*!

It makes me sick to hear the "news." A sole starving animal is forced out of its "home," its habitat, while maybe just out of hibernation and in a desperate search for food, maybe a few berries. This is reported as a "bear stalked, cornered, or tried to viciously attack" some person who was not even touched or harmed. The bear is shot and killed. For what? Searching for food to eat or to feed its cubs? This is repeated every single day. There are no "safe zones" for any animal since we have taken over every inch of the planet. It "belongs" to us. They can't have access to it or any food.

We venture out of our natural world into the water, where a person "is viciously attacked" by a shark. Really? Their home? We don't live there. We can't survive in the water. But every inch of that is "ours" exclusively. Despite millions of species that live in the water, their home, we continue to dump every type of garbage, pollutant, chemicals and toxins imaginable. The millions of marine life kept it perfectly balanced and pristine for billions of years, maintaining that balance for all to live and survive. Until one arrived and destroyed it for marine life, us, and the planet.

There is no "out there." Everything dumped, spilled, and tossed is still here, in the home where we all live, on land, sea or wherever. It is like living in a home with all your children and grandchildren. Never opening your door, having no toilet, just dumping everything you use, every single day straight into your house. That is disgusting, and no one would survive for very long. It will not look, smell, or be pristine.

Dumping waste into oceans ingested by animals.

Unlike us, nature manages to reabsorb every living thing, matter, or biodegradable waste back into the ecosystem. Pristine, clean, and safe, for billions of years. No one species is having to take sole responsibility for doing it. It is a perfect self-sustaining system that cannot be improved upon. That blueprint we need to follow. Nature is a Fair System.

Unlike all other species that live within the "win-win" model, why are humans the only species that does not seem able to comprehend that we, too, must live this way? It is not an accident or coincidence that all life on the planet operates this way. It is proven with absolute certainty to be the most successful system to maximize the survival of all species and, in particular, the survival of the planet. The earth does not operate on a class system, on have or have nots, rich or poor, educated or not, based on gender or race or species, for that matter. Nature is the fairest system and provides for all and to the greatest numbers of all. It matters not to the planet that humans have devised arbitrary and unfair or unjust ways of living. The planet does not react in an immediate manner to threats upon it, since in nature, changes occur relatively slowly and naturally so that the eco-system is able to adapt to these changes. This is critical to the balance that maintains itself very successfully. In nature, all species only utilize things that occur naturally within the environment. Nature is not designed for, nor does it function successfully, in a manner that humans have decided to live. There is no "win-win" for the earth or any species to adjust to, and balance itself against the total warfare humans have waged against it. It has never had to. Why would any species want to destroy its life source? None do. Why are we? The earth has been put into a bizarre reality of "fighting for its own survival." The earth has attempted utilizing the ever-successful strategy of gradual adaptation and rebalance, but for the first time, it would appear this is unsuccessful. So over time, humans have actively obstructed Earth's attempts to stabilize life and its ecosystem. Rather than observe and learn from the successful natural systems in place, humans decided nature was mismanaging the planet. Obviously, our narcissistic nature claims that not only are we are the superior species on the planet but that we are also the preferred one to survive above all others. Of course, we intentionally delude ourselves by maintaining this self-serving belief because it allows us to justify waging war on the planet. All one must do to dispel this delusion is to look at how we are destroying the planet to know. Earth would never support such a strategy for living or survival because it is not, has never been, can never be, successful.

The Human Need to Manage

Humans, for some reason, take something that "is not broken" and decide to fix it. Once we started doing this, it became a total mess. Where all things were perfectly balanced and sustaining, we started "managing things." We have an infinite number of departments: Fisheries and Oceans, Wildlife Management, Parks and Recreation. We began to "manage" things, and it has become unmanageable, from pollution and deforestation to denying sufficient sources of food or killing various animals we decided there should be more or less of. One year there are too many wolves. They are killed off. Now there will be too many rodents, so we poison them. Eagles eat the poisoned rodents, and now they are killed off. And on, and on. We are managing every single species on the planet literally to death when we only need to start managing one, *us*.

We need to stop overpopulating and over-consuming food sources. We need to stop developing every inch of land to put up concrete structures that cannot sustain any other life. Such structures include housing for humans, malls, playgrounds, theatres, car lots, golf courses, ski mountains, recreation centres, and anything we desire. We keep building more, even though there are usually plenty of them. We don't need to have everything on every block. Even though people spend hours a day going to the gym or working out to stay "fit and healthy," apparently it is too far to walk a few blocks to get things we usually want more than need. This is what we have replaced nature and all our co-inhabitants with. The inhabitants we need to survive are replaced with cold, sterile concrete jungles. Structures that give nothing back. Really, are all these malls that necessary that they are worth exterminating species over, so we don't have to walk one block? This is destructive and does the opposite of sustaining life on the planet. With millions shopping online, do we need hundreds of miles of strip malls? Why are we not tearing these down so the earth can reclaim at least some space for itself, nature, and some animals and plants to resurface—trees, plants, and life forms that will help clean the air we need to breathe. The oxygen provided by trees and plants nurtures us and our soul. There is lots of research showing our health and well-being are replenished and healed when we are "in nature" or with animals.

Unsustainable overdevelopment.

It is not enough to have tiny, human-manufactured lakes, parks, or reserves, which were home to many species. Raccoons, coyotes, or eagles, better not cross our path in "our park or areas," or they might have to be killed. For the species that considers itself most dominant, powerful, and superior, we seem to have limited response to everything: kill it, destroy it, cage it. Why are we treating all species with such hostility? They wish us no harm. Every day, we see stories of amazing bonds between humans and many different types of wildlife. Some animals have been tortured and have lived in captivity their whole lives. They don't attack. They show a tremendous capacity to still trust and love. Living beings should not be sold or trafficked for money or profit. Just as it is wrong—criminal—to traffic human beings and, children, so should it include every living species. Species need to live in their natural habitat to live successfully and to contribute to the ecosystem.

How would humans fare if an animal abducted us and decided we should live with it underground, underwater, or on the branch of a tree for the remainder of our life? It's preposterous, cruel and inhumane. Animals are not toys to keep in our homes. Birds are not for caging. No animal should be caged. It should not be legal or allowed.

Beauty and joy of birds in flight.

The Problem of Entitlement

Early humans looked to the stars to understand their world. More recently, it seems people are turning their focus on a smaller and smaller target. We have gone from gazing at the stars and exploring the land, oceans, society, community, family, and single-parent family to the last single target, ourselves or the individual—the "me" generation. The planet is not designed to meet individual needs or rather wants. No system can. No one species can be all-powerful and all-important. Neither can humans as a species. We definitely can't as individuals. We can try to understand ourselves and our needs, but we can't just live in our own heads 24/7.

What humans used to gaze upon to understand the world around them.

It can't be all about "me," my wants, my selfies, my fifteen minutes of fame. And if I don't have what I want, then I take it by force. What gives anyone the right to rob someone because they want something? We don't need most manufactured material things to survive. It is not a basic need. Kill someone for their money or car or whatever to feed an addiction or hoarding. We just continue to lower the bar, accept immoral, unethical, or criminal behaviour.

Some parents will defend their child's violence, bullying, or anger. Some parents have gone as far as to break the law intentionally to meet the demands of their children, to get into a school, or become a cheerleader. I recall an example of a mother who was actually selling herself to buy her teenage daughter a car. The teenager complained the car was "not brand new." This is how parents and adults are creating entitled, and in many cases, sociopathic behaviours in society. This is the future unless people start understanding how to raise healthy children who become healthy adults. They will create havoc on everyone and the planet when they realize the world is not the way they want or expect it should be. Children must start spending way less time on unproductive and counterproductive games and in taking selfies. This is wasted time and gives the illusion that nothing needs to change and there is nothing different they or you need to be doing. This is not the truth. Children of a young age are able to be more involved and even want to be helpful. Everyone needs to play their part. There are serious consequences for inadequate, inappropriate parenting. It should be everyone's business.

We need to start spending less time obsessing about ourselves and our own wants. This is the last strategy that we need when we and the planet are on the verge of total collapse. We need to broaden our focus on what we need, not as individuals but as humans, if we want to stay alive on the planet.

Stop feeding into the "it's all about me" mentality. That's what got us into the mess we are in right now. We need to get back to focusing on how we are going to breathe, get clean water and food to eat, and make the world healthier and safer for all, now and in the future. We need to unplug from all our devices, chats, games, and attention-seeking and get back to helping the world survive our assault and neglect of it—time to unplug and wake up. If people want things to do, there is a planet to save. So, we need to "just do it."

It's time to Stop. Look. Listen. It's not working. It's getting worse. We need to stop destroying the planet. We need a whole new system. Not more of the one that wasn't working. We can't be this dense, can we? Do people want all life to end? If not, why aren't we stopping it? Have we become this lazy, uncaring, apathetic, and uncreative that no one can think of how to do things differently? The superior, dominant, powerful species in the planet, capable of destroying the planet, can't figure out how to raise a healthy generation? Parents, help your children by leading and helping them to a better path—brainstorm sessions with family and friends.

Young people can start organizing with their friends and fellow students how to put pressure on the local officials. Ask tough questions about the lack of adequate protection of the planet and its future. Children used to earn money by cutting their neighbour's lawn. Now they just get everything (on their parent's credit card) and are spending hours a day on their devices, playing games, chatting, or posting selfies. This is the arena that fuels the consumption because they all want the next new thing that their friends or the Kardashians have. They are spending too much time in isolation and losing a lot of social skills and etiquette, just as they are losing their ability to spell because of texting and spell-check. When the internet is down, many cannot do the math to make change at the checkout because they cannot do math longhand. Too many kids are not learning how to do many things that were considered very basic. Parents have a duty and obligation to teach their children how to be independent, self-reliant and resourceful. They won't be able to move out on their own without knowing how to cope and solve daily problems, tasks, or issues. Kids have broken into a home to charge their phone or have gone to an office to get their phone charged. This has become synonymous with "survival." This is ridiculous and feeds into the notion they only need technology to "live or survive" when nothing is further from the truth. Teach and love your kids. Don't "buy" them. Kids want items so bad, so desperately that they are stealing them, or someone is bullied or beating someone for them. Parents need to do a better job at instilling the values, the compass, if you will. If parents don't have a compass, they can't teach it to their children. This is why many in society seem to be "lost." They are not sure what they are doing or supposed to be focusing on or making a priority. We need a compass. When you have to walk five miles for water, you know what you are doing it for: to survive. We have become too far removed from that and now confuse things as being necessary for "survival." This has to change. Let's first look at what the subtle and not-so-subtle obstacles might be.

Preoccupation with smart devices.

THE PONZI SCHEME ECONOMY AND CORPORATE DICTATORSHIP

Representing a Pyramid Model or Ponzi Scheme.

Ponzi Scheme Defined

The politicians are running the economy based on the pyramid Ponzi scheme (like Madoff). So is the corporate financial model. They need an ever-increasing base, which means increasing the population to keep the system going. The larger growing base at the bottom pays for the fewer on the top. Everyone knows this is a con, and this always goes bust. It is not sustainable, but the few on top take everyone's money and run. They do not care about the carnage they leave behind. While people lose their pensions and savings and are maybe left penniless and homeless, the con artist continues living on millions or billions, free of remorse, guilt and, too often, of consequences. This is the corporate, Wallstreet mentality. Elected officials are not supposed to run the government this way. But like all of us, they are trapped in an economic system based on unlimited growth. They will not start telling the people the truth: that the economy cannot sustain the unlimited growth of human beings. Every year it is the same discussion, not enough funds for schools, daycare, hospital beds, affordable housing, care homes, mental health workers, police officers, and highways. Every year the infrastructure is overburdened and unable to meet the immediate needs of its citizens or communities, every service bulging at the seams, every single year. Don't look at the elected officials and the corporate world. They do not have an interest in protecting people or the planet. Why? Democracy has been replaced by corporate dictatorship.

How the wealthy live from our consumerism and consumption of the planet.

How much of humanity lives now and will be in increasing numbers due to consumerism and unchecked human overpopulation.

Corporate Driven Consumerism and Population

No one dare say the "obvious." The planet, all the cities we have created, big or small, can not, and will never be able to absorb, the almost 400,000 people being added to the planet *every single day.* It is time to say this. Every species that has managed to survive has done so by balancing its population. They do not even have to pay for anything. They put in, and they take out. All in balance.

With all our superior capabilities, humans must spend billions, trillions every year, only to have the same, or worse, conditions the next year. What kind of system is this, and why do billions allow them to keep doing it?

Humans, it's time to wake up! We need to get off this "consume and populate" lie that we have been sold and we have accepted. The corporate world is never going to suggest we make fewer people and consume less. No, they keep upping the ante. It is not enough you have a pair of Nike shoes. Now you "need" one in every colour. You must change your cell phone for a new model, even though the one you have, works fine, and is paid off. There will never be an endpoint where you can ever say, "I have everything, and I don't need more." The corporate and advertising world will never let you say that. That would represent a failure on their part. The mistake most people make is allowing themselves to confuse wants with needs. Of course, this is what advertising and marketing are all about. You must confuse these. Otherwise, you will figure out you do not need most of these things, and you surely do not need more of them. If you run out of money, they won't let you stop.

If you do not have the cash, no problem, you can add another credit card to the other ones that are already maxed out. Or you can buy furniture, but not pay the balance for two years. Or just get another loan or line of credit. Do anything, but do not stop buying. So off people go, to work harder, longer hours. Their money does not go very far, and they are drowning in debt. They cannot quit their job; maybe they hate it, but they cannot take a chance. So, they are trapped.

This is the role we get to play. We get to buy our way to our own demise, the demise of our children and the planet. All the trees that give us oxygen and species that allow us to live are being exterminated so humans can keep expanding to put trillions of dollars into the hands of the wealthy. This is where your purchases and credit card debt go to: the destruction of life. Your life. This is what we have become, co-conspirators to the destruction of the planet. Go shop. "Help the economy." You are not helping the economy. You are helping make the rich richer.

If consuming was the answer to making the economy better, stronger, wealth "trickling down," why are things getting worse for people? Why are so many people having to work three jobs at fast-food chains? Should you not be able to afford a house? Should you be maxed out on your credit cards? Should your adult kids not be able to move out? Afford to even rent a place? Is there evidence that the economy is being helped and you are being helped? It's not a lack of consumerism. So, what? It is a lie. Spending money and buying things makes rich people richer. It makes other people money. It does not help you or your financial situation or future. Don't listen to the propaganda.

The media will not tell you any of this. Think about this. Is there any coverage of these issues? I would think this to be critical information to "educate" us. "Inform" us. Is that not what the "news" is supposed to do? *No.* Listen to it every day, but you will never hear about these issues. The things that impact our life and future and what solutions there might be *never* discussed or covered by politicians or the media. They have become instruments of the powerful corporate world. They have become omnipotent. They have become the new "religion." Religion was considered the "opiate of the people." Now the media is "the opiate of the people." Where once religion told people how to live, it is now corporations through media that tell you how to live. It always involves getting everyone into their "consumer trap." It entraps billions every day to keep buying products. Look beautiful so that you can find the "one true love." Then next is the "get married trap," then the "having a family trap," a big house, car, and a couple with children—all one big happy family. The cost of weddings has become more extravagant for average-income people. The cost of having children is outrageous. The cost of having a house, out of most people's reach. And a "happy" couple often does not survive these traps, and some are divorced before the wedding has even been paid for. Unless they have parents, who have paid, it is on their credit card. Not a healthy situation to begin life with a new partner or to add dependants to. Is it a wonder so many fail? But for the corporate world, this is perfect. These "traps" are put out 24/7 all around you, and it is only a matter of time before you get snagged again. More profit for the corporations again. Your failure is their success. No matter what.

We control the population, and we control the corporate world. They will be so desperate for consumers, their products will have to meet our needs, our prices, with increased quality. Billions of us need to learn we don't "need" products. We need healthy children, a healthy future, and a healthy planet. Stop buying disposable products. Stop buying live Christmas trees and throwing them out like garbage. This is how we teach children to use and abuse nature. Trees keep us alive. No trees and plants, no oxygen.

We can make a decision not to have children or have one or two and stop buying things we don't need. Corporations control the population by making us all slaves. Cheap labour. More overpopulation, more slave labour and people living in destitute conditions. I am not talking about the developing nations. I am talking about North America. It has already started happening.

The Declining Standard of Living

Everyone can notice their standard of living going down. My parents were lower-middle class with mostly one income. They bought a house, had a car, went on vacation and had five kids. Now a two-income couple with no kids is facing challenges buying a home. Young people used to be able to move out and have a full-time job at sixteen years of age. No high school or Grade 12. They had a good income and were independent. When I was young, only teens would have a job at McDonald's in the summer or on weekends to make some spending money. Now single parents are working these low-level jobs as their "career." In the US, some people have three or four jobs working casual hours because the corporations do not have to pay any benefits to casual employees. They all make more money off your hard work and give you less money and benefits in return. Stop supporting this Ponzi scheme. The only people who want this to continue are the corporations. Why do jobs go overseas? The same reason, cheap labour. Why is labour cheap in those countries? Guess. Overpopulation. Extreme poverty. You don't have to be a mathematician to figure out that you, we, are becoming that country. This is what having as many kids as you want does to the economy and your community, and your children's future. This is what allowing corporations to run the world does.

You see that young people cannot move out of their parents' home anymore. They can't even afford a car or make car payments. Cars cost more than what houses used to cost. My parents bought a beautiful custom-built home for $25,000. Parents are saving to pay for their children's post-secondary education and, if lucky, a down payment for a condo for their adult child. What will life be like for their children? They will not have the funds to support their children's education. If, as a parent, you have your adult kids living with you now, how will they raise their children in a rented condo? Or, if they cannot move out and need to stay at home, things are going to get very cramped for space and strapped for cash. They cannot afford a car now. What will their kids be able to afford?

This is how North America is joining the rest of the world. But in order to make sure, people don't start noticing their standard of living is in sharp decline, and God forbid, start having smaller families or saving money and not spending, they have to keep giving you more credit and loan options. This way, everyone has the illusion that life is good and prosperous.

Planned Obsolescence

The products we buy don't last a lifetime like they used to. Part of the plan and strategy is to make cheap items that don't last, so you have to keep buying. This is called planned obsolescence, a more recent corporate culture because, at one time, the hallmark of a good company was a product "was made to last." You bought an appliance, and it lasted you a lifetime. If it broke down, a representative from the store or company came right out and fixed it. What happens now? You pay lots of money for an appliance. They sell it, then wash their hands. You pay for an extra "warranty" for a product that will last a few years if you are lucky. If you have a problem, don't call the store. They have nothing to do with you anymore. Now you have to spend hours or days on the phone trying to hold the manufacture or company accountable. The run-around you get is designed to make you give up, even though your appliance is not working, and you paid extra for a warranty. So, you accept a faulty appliance, or you call someone and pay for that service yourself. No savings really.

The reason the stores and companies can do this is because they don't care about the customer. They now rely on mass consumers, not repeat customers. We all get the short end of the stick, and the companies make more money. They don't have to face the customer because it is all online or by phone. This is your Ponzi scheme at work. They are interested in high volume, not quality or customer satisfaction. They do it because we keep buying. What would happen if people said, "Well, we are not buying poor quality products or services anymore?" The companies and corporations would be forced to improve. We are being fooled with so-called savings and low costs. What we are getting is low-quality goods that are meant to be disposable so that the consumer or "victim" of the Ponzi scheme has to keep purchasing the same substandard products, so in a sense, you are a repeat consumer as well. Take notice of things you buy all the time. The packaging is bigger, but the contents are smaller—the canned goods, pop cans, bottles, all skinner and smaller. Toilet rolls—not as many or smaller. This is going on all the time over decades. We keep getting less and paying more. The corporations and marketing people are counting their trillions. Meanwhile, what is the so-called consumer protection of the government doing? Where are our taxes going when so many departments are doing nothing for us with the taxes we pay? This goes on in every department in government. Like the corporations, they take our money and give us very little, if anything. This has been going on for decades. This is one of the reasons our money is not going as far as it used to. We pay more for purchases and in taxes but can't afford to buy more than the minimum every month. Forget buying a house or car.

And the other victim in the scheme is the person doing the "slave labour." This is coming to a city near you. These conditions are becoming global, and there is no escaping them. If you want your children to have a chance at a better life, rather than where they are headed right now, things need to change. We need to change. We need to put politicians who are supporting the corporations out of work. We need to put these corporations and companies out of work. We need to prevent the continued exploitation of children (and adults) as they will be used for slave labour. Human and child trafficking exists only because of overpopulation and extreme poverty. We need to stop being robots. Stop being manipulated and lied to, brainwashed into "shopping till we drop," or getting married and having kids as a default plan for everyone on the planet. *Stop* being a helpless victim of the Ponzi scheme. Politicians don't care enough, and they are controlled by the mega-corporations. Wake up, call people. We must curb our expansion on the planet because every jump in population means there is less earth to support life, and increased suffering for those on it.

The Cost of Having a Family

Maybe some can't really afford to get married or have any children. But the world bombards people with the fantasy of marriage. It's no coincidence that weddings are one of the biggest profit-making industries, but the one to surely follow is even bigger. That is the baby industry—the most expensive for people but the most profitable for corporations. Babies have designer lines of clothes, shoes, everything one can imagine. It does not matter if they grow so fast that they can only wear them a couple of times. All the better, as a fast-growing child continues to need items, and that is great for the corporate world. They do not care if you are in debt up to your eyeballs.

The media is a 24/7 consumer show, meant to serve as some "expert" that brainwashes kids and parents alike that they "need" or "must" have certain items. Kids often play with a toy and never look at it again. But the toys keep coming. Not all are being charitable and recycling them to other families locally or around the globe to children who have zero toys to play with. So, into the landfill, they go. Of course, the "landfill" was home to thousands of species that have been displaced or exterminated so we can dump our ever-increasing non-biodegradable garbage. But with the Ponzi scheme economy we created, there must be more babies, and there must be more buying. This cannot be slowed down because the fear is that there will be a "total collapse" of the economy. This is what the corporate world wants you to believe. This is what the politicians either believe or, because they receive huge contributions or "bribes" from the corporate heads, they have to deliver the same message. The politicians don't really want to put in the effort it would take to change the economy from a Ponzi scheme to a sustainable one. Remember, they are not "leaders" but are actually followers of the money. Why should they risk anything, money or popularity and their elected position, by doing the right thing? They don't have the required "internal compass" that should act as a deterrent from doing unethical things. This compass should ensure they do the right thing for the people and the planet.

People need to stop being pawns in this Ponzi scheme. Stop being pawns in this economy based on having children and more children regardless of whether you want any or can afford any more. This is not to suggest that people are not able to afford the child(ren) they have, or that they are in any way dependent on assistance of any kind, though plenty are. The issue is we must look beyond our individual wants and desires by taking into consideration the state and needs of the planet, what the planet can sustain. If someone wants the privilege of being a parent, they can have that experience. But having more than one or two increases the population, which is already unsustainable now. There are millions of children ready to be adopted. The infrastructure already burst. We cannot continue with the destruction of the planet, trees, plants, animals and biodiversity to accommodate near half a million more babies a day.

What remedies are being presented? None? The biggest problem that is threatening our survival and that of the planet, and there are none? The fact there no one is presenting anything, or at least nothing that is being covered in the media and by politicians, should be a clue. The power of the corporations, the con of the Ponzi scheme, and the backlash by powerful people, corporate people, have made it clear this is not to be discussed. It is the most taboo subject universally. Even environmental organizations won't touch it. Everyone goes around it, saying, "Save the trees," "save the oceans," "save the whales," save the wildlife," "save the tigers," "save the Amazon jungle," "save the bees," "save the climate," even though the number one solution to *all* these problems is one: Reduce human population, and thereby consumption.

Yes, China had a one-child policy to put some control on its population expansion. The problem is that their population was already allowed to expand far beyond what was sustainable for their resources, and it was absolutely devastating to the planet. It didn't necessarily prevent people from having another child, but it did result in the practice of female infanticide for couples to deal with the one-child policy. Others hid subsequent pregnancies or babies. Ironically, but not surprising, these policies ultimately lead to an extreme shortage of females for the males to marry and continue their lineage. Some female babies and children were abducted or bought by wealthy people to secure a wife for their son. This is again an example of a human, self-inflicted problem, because rather than follow nature's blueprint, we are forever trying to manipulate the sustainable process to meet the "needs" of the mutant culture.

The Cost of Overpopulation

Why is there such little coverage and discussion of this issue? We should be very suspicious of this silence. Talk about the proverbial "elephant in the room." Why is everyone skirting around, over, under this one issue? Why can *no one* touch this? Why is the one off-limits? The silence is deafening. Listen. Hear it! Question why this is so. Why can we not talk about population and how it is playing a role in the degradation of the economy and standard of living? How can this not be relevant? We blame the seals when there is a shortage of fish. How can billions of us, and growing, not have an impact on the planet's resources and ecosystem?

Reducing population is the one issue that every single one of us can directly impact negatively or positively. Each person can choose more earth-friendly family planning options, for some not to have any children, others maybe one or two. Out of all the issues like "save this and save that," billons can actually change this. Immediately. That is exciting and incredible. How can I possibly save the tiger when billions are destroying their habitat so people can take over their territory? How can I save the elephants when the consumer demand for ivory is not eliminated? As long as more people need more land and greed feeds this Ponzi scheme economy, there is no saving anything. That is incredibly depressing and makes me feel hopeless because nothing is improving in any way. Yet if a billion out of eight billion decided they were not having kids or eight billion decided they would have one child, imagine that impact? That would be astronomical. It takes no effort. (It is estimated that China's controversial one-child policy prevented up to 400 million births and reduced China's birthrate to 1.7)

Contraception use for men and women is available. Instead of trying to save each species, one at a time, we need to invest in education and contraception. The best way not to allow this Ponzi scheme to continue to destroy us is to take control of our reproductive and contraception options. This is the only way the planet is going to be saved. Nature knows it is the only way humanity and the planet can be saved. If the Ponzi scheme is allowed to push for 400,000 babies a day, there is *no* hope for our survival, your children's children, nor the planet.

Nature's Birth Control

Nature continues attempting to balance human population, but the mutant culture will not allow it. We defy, resist, and obstruct. Nature responds to all the conditions in the ecosystem by impacting our reproductive systems. They are the most sensitive to environmental and prenatal conditions. It is no coincidence that after decades of dumping harmful chemicals right up to today that nature is trying to do what is needed to rebalance. Sperm counts and fertility rates have taken a steady dive. But we say, "no way." We will not listen to or follow nature's blueprint. Fertility treatments are not just allowing a child to be born but allowing for multiple births. Now someone can have six or eight babies at one time. No one tries to talk anyone out of this. In fact, there are shows that celebrate multiple births like *Twenty and Counting.* This is not something that needs to be encouraged or celebrated. I don't even know if multiple births should be an option. Sure, if there was ever a danger of critical under-population it could be introduced. But currently, with overpopulation, should this be a "right"?

Conversely, a woman, who wants to prevent pregnancy through a procedure, such as tubal ligation, is discouraged or even denied if she is "too young or single." In 2021, men have but one available primary contraception, which most don't like—a condom. With overpopulation being so critical, one would think contraception for men would be given a much higher priority. By default, society makes it very difficult not to have children. But how about caring for them? It's not just about personal expense or cost. Even if wealthy people can afford many children, how about the impact on the planet, the ever-growing need for increased infrastructure? More land under development for each to have their own mega home. More mass consumption. Yachts, planes, cars on the road, their kids having kids. It is simply not an equation that can work. Just like in nature, we need to follow the blueprint in place. Look at what other species have done to ensure their survival and that of their offspring. They only pass on traits to their offspring that maximize their chances for survival. And they maintain a balance between birth and available resources. It happens naturally in the biological laws of nature.

Continued Destruction

These wealthy people are already planning their disposal of the Earth and all life by their exploration of other planets. Don't think it is possible in our lifetime or ever to escape to another planet. Earth has evolved for billions of years to give all life the optimum conditions to survive and thrive. There will be no other options. This is an illusion to further deceive the multitudes of us that we don't need to protect the planet, we will just throw the Earth away as a disposable product, and all eight billion of us can go live on another planet. This is a lie, science fiction. They are planning to make money from destroying the planet by selling tickets to take trips to the Moon or Mars. This gives us the illusion that this is how we will all be saved—more money for wealthy people to make off of us while doing more destruction to the planet. There is an idea that people can start travelling on Earth, from city to city, on rockets instead of airplanes. More money for the wealthy and more destruction of the planet. We have to stop this insane "merry-go-round" of destruction. If the planet is destroyed, the wealthy will be able to construct their own self-sustaining bubbles wherever they might be. They will use their wealth to provide whatever they require to live in luxury. This will not be available to any of us. They will continue to be well-protected and guarded. They will have made themselves rulers of the planet and beyond. Now, if that's not narcissistic and hedonistic, nothing is. That is dangerous if allowed to continue.

We accept these warnings, such as poor air quality advisory, meaning don't go out to breathe the air we need to live and survive. That could kill us. There are still other advisories such as boil or don't drink the water, water that we can't live without and need to survive. No problem. It's poisoned, so we can pay for it. Despite it being provided by nature, clean and free for billions of years, now we have to pay the corporations billions of dollars to drink bottled water. Do you think this encourages them to protect the environment when they know, not only do we not protest and demand clean water, but we also just line up to pay them to get water that was clean before they polluted it? What a scam. If anything, this encourages these corporations to continue to destroy the planet because we have allowed them to profit from it. Our money is being used this way. Where is our activism? Our compass? For us, the children, their future and the planet? People displace their outrage over parking spots or rants at others over petty things or products. But for poisoning us, killing us and the planet, we have no response, no outrage? What is wrong with us mutants? Why do we accept this? Why are we not out by the millions, by the billions demanding the richest people, companies, and worst perpetrators of this mass killing and destruction be held accountable? Is this not "crimes against humanity?"

Since corporations, politicians, and the media, have started ruling us and the planet, they have put us on a homicidal-suicidal path. They have made us their co-conspirators in the violence against each other and the planet.

Countering Destruction

We must demand that elected officials actually fast-track issues of a critical nature—life and death issues facing the planet. We already saw the world do it during the Covid-19 crisis. No one thought it possible to come up with a life-saving vaccine so fast. Never mind more than one. But we saw it could be done because all areas, government, researchers, and the corporate world came together and did it at lightning speed. It can and must be done. Usually, we are told there are not enough funds (taxes), and yet it got done. Corporations (not all) got a taste of what can happen to their bottom line when people can't shop, go to restaurants, or go on vacation. They saw it and did not like it. So, corporations did the "right thing" only because they had no choice. It was self-protection. But we learned how *not* shopping can hurt them, and we must not forget this. We tell them we will not buy their goods unless we get better quality, green products, and they clean the mess they made of the planet. Period. We can't afford decades of lack of action, delays, clogged up in the system. It should not be permitted that politicians and lawmakers let life-threatening conditions continue for decades without a single bit of progress. The corporations are allowed to keep dumping poisons and toxins into the air, water, and food sources, making millions sick with progressive diseases, cancers, and death. Why are we not outraged?

It is time for a global pushback. A revolution as many we have had before. When enough people unite together for a common purpose, change can happen. We have to fight against this powerful corporate tsunami that has taken control of our lives, our children's future, our money and the planet. This planet does not belong to anyone, no corporation. This planet is to share and live with all the other species that need the same things they and we never had to pay for.

We need to put protection of the planet, not its destruction, as our number one priority. The earth, air, water, plants, soil, food, and other species are not "products." They need to be protected so humanity can survive. The earth was abundant for billions of species for billions of years. Never running out, getting poisoned or destroyed or depleted. We must unite globally and put a stop to this suicidal mission we are all on.

We can no longer be passive. It can no longer be "business as usual." We need to make ourselves more independent of this "corporate dictatorship." This must be overthrown. Like any violent dictator's regime, it must be toppled. We need to remember we and this planet did just fine before we allowed corporations to rule the planet. We need to get that back. Can we allow ourselves to become better neighbours and a better community? We can reach out and help each other—reduce the practice to buy things individually that we can share use of. Why is it we "need" to buy a lawnmower when nature was already doing this? Use a push lawnmower. It is better for the environment and good exercise—one less trip to the gym. Can't some things be allowed to just grow? Instead of putting up fences, let nature provide the privacy, the shade. Plant shrubs, trees, and fruit trees. There are many animals that eat grass. People can get creative if they must have some grass. "Rent a sheep" for the day, and they can eat it all up. A win-win start-up. Some cities have started introducing nature back into solving problems. We can have a community co-op. When someone needs a lawnmower, get it from the co-op. Everyone contributes items they have to the co-op, so everyone does not need to buy them. Plant community gardens for more fresh food to share. Plant fruit trees. Plant things that promote survival for bees and other pollinators.

That is what nature practices, a win-win. Why are we "fixing" things that are not broken? Why do we use noisy, polluting machines when there are animals dying to eat grass? No use of harmful chemicals. No harm to the planet. This is one out of thousands of examples of how we can save money, buy fewer products, and protect the environment.

The Power of Community

Within communities, there are many examples of how to live better. People have started to carpool. We can share resources within communities with our neighbours that might have things others can use and vice versa. Would this not be a better way to live than everyone sitting alone in isolation or in fear of their neighbours? In times of tragedy, neighbours come out to help each other. We need to be able to rely on each other. Could our lives not get better if we could get our sense of community back? We could do things of mutual benefit and save money. Conditions and standards of living are coming down; there is no denying it. So, if people want to avoid creating hostile, tense communities where everyone protects what they have and do not reach out, we will then create the same situation of "haves and have nots." Let's get back to being better people, neighbours, and communities. Would children not be better off and grow up healthier if they had families and neighbours to help if parents need some short-term support, rather than rely on an agency or ever-dwindling services. No agency can look after every child in every area. The community must provide some helping hands. We all suffer if children are abused and neglected. Will some of them end up feeling resentful or robbing your house to feed an addiction? We all pay the price for harm done to other people and the planet. There is no win-win. Only lose-lose. What are we going to do to change this head-on disaster we are facing?

Learning from the Pandemic

It will take some time, but if Covid-19 has taught us anything, it is that we can go a long way without doing things or shopping all the time. And despite the mantra by politicians, things can be accomplished and fast when there is the will. Not one politician said we need more data, research, surveys, have more meetings, or that they can't afford to get it done. So, we have this evidence, locally and globally, that things get done. Now we need to apply this same demand and method to clean and protect the planet like driving our cars less, eating in more often and saving money, which we need for the next time there is another pandemic, and there will be. We also saw a measurable and visible improvement in the air quality from fewer cars on the road. Wildlife came back into areas it had not been in for decades. This is proof that what we do can either be harmful or helpful. Given a chance, nature bounces back relatively quickly. We can improve the air quality by letting nature come back to doing what she does best—nurture life. More trees will clean the air and protect us from the wind and sun. They will keep the soil stronger to reduce slides and flooding, not to mention the millions of other species that call the tree home and food. All the while, these creatures mind their own business, harming nothing and certainly not us or the planet. I would rather invest in this ecosystem than our destructive financial system. One gives us life; the other destroys it.

We need to learn the lessons from this pandemic. Many local businesses went under, which is a tragedy. Our local neighbours lost their livelihoods. But the mega corporations got bigger and wealthier. Now they are no longer billionaires but trillionaires. We did not have these before. So, we need to get back to supporting each other in every way in our communities. Covid has proven what can be done. We must save humanity and the planet and not let up that demand.

Learning to Curb Spending.

Parents need to set the example—no more obsessive buying online. If kids want something, parents have to be better role models. If it is not needed, maybe it should not be purchased. Do young children really "need" manicures, pedicures? Do adults?

After all, they are inheriting the mess that we created. We need to turn this around because the kids nor we will be able to buy our way to a safer, better future or planet. It does not serve kids to be accustomed to getting anything they "want." They are not going to have the purchasing power of their parents. That is why they are not moving out of your homes now, after becoming adults. So, when you are no longer alive, they will be living a harsh reality. Help them prepare financially and ecologically. Educate them about what is needed to do their part, hopefully, together as a family.

Corporations don't want you to have any time to be organized or active. They want to keep you busy (managing your ever-decreasing pay) with your jobs, children, diapers to change, mouths to feed, taking the children to incessant activities, and bills to pay.

It is important to teach your children that it is not cool to want everything because it's like "blood money." Getting something off the suffering of others.

Starting the Process

We need to have real leaders and willing participants to begin this process. Every one of us needs the planet so every one of us needs to get involved. If we lived in a part of the world where we had to walk ten miles to find food or water, I can assure you, people would not be spending all day on their devices. Our basic needs will soon make that obsolete. A frivolous luxury it is in comparison to air, water, and food. So, we can easily do without these and most things that we have been tricked into believing we can't.

We need to get unplugged and off the devices and constant voices of the media telling us to fear our neighbours, keep to ourselves, buy more things, and have more kids. We need to stop buying things that are not biodegradable and are going to clutter the natural world with garbage. We can't plant this garbage and grow food. All it does is prevent the planet from maintaining its balance.

We need leaders to show the way to get our survival back on track. Remember that all the greatest leaders in the world were *not* elected officials. Think about Gandhi,

Mandala, Martin Luther King, Gloria Steinem, Malala Yousafzai, or our youngest leader, Greta Thunberg. She is a leader in the truest sense. We must have more young, tenacious, tireless people like her joining the global movement for a better world. She is a mentor for anyone looking for one. She has the integrity and courage that others (elected or not) lack. She has put herself on the line, and just like others before her, is subjected to backlash, violence, and hate. She must not be silenced, and people need to strengthen her voice and act in support of her behavior. She does not need a pat on the back. She needs more people to demand the changes. The people who changed the world are everyday people, young and old, people who cared enough to stand up and do what is right.

This is a pivotal moment in history and for our future. It is critical for our survival that this corporate machinery be dismantled. Let's put our money and actions into only things that will help make the planet cleaner, healthier, and safer.

DANGEROUS LIAISONS. CORPORATIONS, POLITICIANS, AND MEDIA-A CONSPIRACY OF MISINFORMATION, DECEIT AND GREED

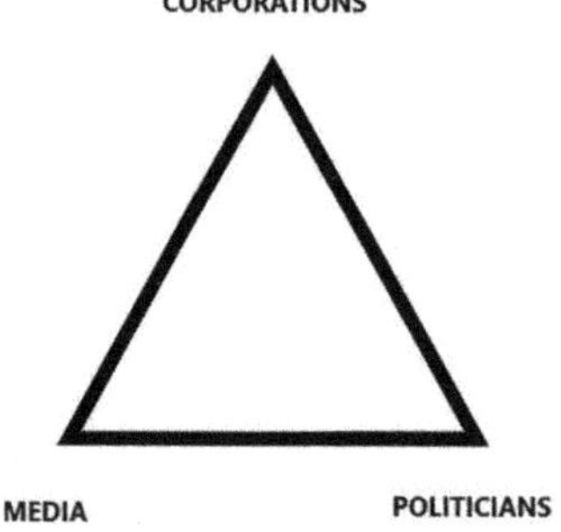

AXIS OF EVIL

Fig. 01 representing "axis of evil' model.

It is time now to be blunt about what is going on and the part we play in maintaining the status quo, which we know, is the destruction of the planet. Having children is not a fantasy life of joy and bliss. That does not mean some parents don't have that with their children. Many do. There are millions who don't, and millions of babies and children who are not cared for, live in harsh poverty, starvation, and are abused and even killed. There are people who should not have had children. But for a variety of reasons, they felt they "needed" them, or they had "no choice." There are many cultures that do "not allow" the use of contraception. This is a self-inflicted human choice that serves to overpopulate, though many cannot afford to raise their children, give them a minimum standard of life, or a healthy, safe future. It is time to admit that these systems are rigidly created and enforced to keep the system afloat. Neither the religious groups nor the corporations seem the least bit concerned that millions of children suffer and die every year, but they continue with their mantra or so-called duty to overpopulate the earth. Neither organization will help financially support all those children they tell you to have. Listen to them, but it all falls on you. This will only result in more children born into more poverty and harsh conditions, which they have no means to escape. So, remember these systems, these mantras, are cages that keep you and billions trapped in this prison to consume and populate, which keeps destroying the planet. The mantra is a voice in union by "the axis of evil"—the dangerous union of corporations, politicians, and the media. The corporation is at the head of the triangle holding all the wealth and power over the other two. The corporation gives plenty of money to politicians and media groups to ensure the corporation maintains its power and wealth. Unfortunately, a majority of politicians chose money over people and the planet. Media groups are not employed investigative journalists but hired personalities to continue to sell and reinforce the corporation's messages and products. They, too, help corporations to maintain their firm grip on their wealth and power—all three acting in concert against people and the planet.

Media

Historically, people have considered the "news" to be an important medium for facts about what is occurring in the world. Families would sit around their radio, and later, their TVs to get their evening news, and it was only once a day that people watched it. Today we are getting "news" twenty-four hours a day.

Where once religion was considered the "opiate of the people," at some point, media, more specifically advertising and consumerism, has replaced it. Shopping has become the new opiate of the people. People are addicted in a very dangerous way. Everything is just a "click" away.

Malls have replaced the church as the place to congregate. With "smart devices" designed to make us think less, allow everyone to feed into these impulses and addictions on a twenty-four-hour basis. Less free-thinking, independent media programs are replaced with programs that give people the illusion they are educating themselves or keeping a focus on what is important. The excuse or justification for the media programming is "that is what sells or what people want." This is completely false and intentionally so. People believe it is important if it is on TV. Not the other way around. If nothing but educational programs were available, people would watch those and become more educated and informed in the process. The "dumbing down" programs are very intentional. The objective is to keep people not thinking, not being aware or informed. But brainwashed to think what they are seeing and hearing on the media and "news" is an accurate reflection of the real world and society.

Most of what I see and hear does not resemble my life, but they do affect people's (adult and especially the young) sense of priorities and "values." People are watching "reality" shows like *The Kardashians*. These women are famous for looking pretty and being wealthy. They don't live lives that reflect any of us. They have no real jobs. They are promoting things that none of us can afford to buy and never will. But that is not the point. These shows are promoting the idea that what they have is what you should want. There is nothing real about them, their looks, their bodies, or their life. It is theatre. Acting. With all the diamonds and clothes, they are not necessarily happy. Their diamonds won't help them if they can't breathe the air or have any water to drink.

I can assure you, if they were desperate for air or water, they would give all their wealth away to have that in exchange. Their money is not what keeps them alive. These shows make the rest of us feel inadequate, like failures; we won't ever be able to have what they have. But we already have true wealth if we have access to air, clean water and can have the freedom to go out and make choices for ourselves. We need to stop valuing things that are meaningless over the treasures we already have. If the

Kardashians were stranded on an island and had no clean water to drink, or it was contaminated and drinking it would kill them, and if they were watching people on a TV show being able to go to a tap and drink clean water, they would envy us. They would watch us and think, "I wish I had their life. All we have is stupid rocks or clothes. It will not keep us healthy or alive. How lucky are people who can drink clean water anytime they want?" Don't confuse what you want with what you need. You will have a more satisfying, happy life once you don't. You can never find contentment or happiness if you are chasing wants. Value the planet. That gives us what we need. You will not see this message on your shows nor hear it on the "news." That is intentional.

Image taken by Arwinder during one of many trips to India. This shows many goats under a gigantic boulder benefiting from

the shade it provides. It is in no danger of toppling over though it looks like it would.

What Should be Newsworthy?

The "news" is not intended to inform us about what is happening in the world. It is designed to *distract* us from what is going on in the world. When have we learned something vital, something important happening in the world that impacts all of us and that we need to do something about on the "news?" Never.

I would think telling us about critical issues like almost 400,000 babies are born every day, *is newsworthy*. Eight billion "disposable" diapers are dumped in the landfill (our home) every single year. I think that *is newsworthy*. That each diaper takes 500 years to break down, not degrade. I think that *is newsworthy*. That the waste in the diaper is supposed to be put down the toilet, but most don't do this. I think that *is newsworthy*. How many harmful substances have been added to our local environment? I think that *is newsworthy*. When was the last of any particular species killed off, made extinct, forever? I think that *is newsworthy*. How much less oxygen is there today, this week, this month, due to the devastation of the Amazon Forest? I think that *is newsworthy*. How many people have been killed trying the protect the land they live on? I think that *is newsworthy*. How many children died of starvation today on the planet? I think that *is newsworthy*. How many people were buried in a cemetery, which is land no longer available to other species? I think that *is newsworthy*. In fact, these are alarming facts that should be "breaking news." You don't hear these. Not once, or once in a blue moon, in passing. No, instead, we hear about the person killed in a car accident. Or a home invasion. Or some other bit of information that serves to distract. Why is a car accident "news?" In what way have I "learned" or been "informed?" What was in the "news report" that I did not know but needed to know or should know?

Image of cemetery.

Might it not be more beneficial for me to learn about an issue I can actually play a role in solving. I can't prevent a random car accident. But If I realize that disposable diapers take *500 years* to break down (this does not mean disappear. It can't because it is not biodegradable), I can decide to choose a cloth diaper. If knowing the impact that one diaper will have in damaging the environment for 500 years, that will affect my kids, their kids and many generations, I can make the more responsible and safer option to stop using disposable diapers.

We live at a time where appliances and many other conveniences give us more leisure time. We have washing machines; we don't have to wash diapers by hand like people may have in the past. Surely this is a small but extremely significant step I could actually take to help keep toxic waste from being dumped. Think about almost 400,000 babies a day being born. How many diapers per day are being disposed of that will be harming the planet for 500 years? It is shocking. If we heard this on the "news" every day, maybe people would start doing the right thing, the responsible thing, and stop using disposable diapers. This is information, concrete, factual information—actual news—that can cause a listener to take personal action to prevent causing harm to the planet. Why are we not hearing this every single day?

Corporations love disposable products—the more billions a day, the better. More money, more profit. Destruction of the planet and future generations? Well, that's collateral damage no one seems to care about and are allowing them to escape responsibility for. Why are they getting away with making these products disposable rather than biodegradable?

We just don't ask, don't question, don't think. We have to switch our brains back on to the "think" setting. Do your own research about the world. Care enough to. You won't hear important things you need to know on the "news."

Don't take my word for it. Watch it for one week and take notes. They start off with "headlines," which is already something you have heard about all day. For example, at present, it will be about vaccines for Covid. Then maybe another top world issue on politics. Then it might go to some local events, like a police incident or crime that occurred. Then maybe someone killed or injured in a car accident. Then a quick look at the weather, which one can look up on their smart device available 24/7. Then a quick recap. Then some coverage of sports events. And maybe what will be coming up on the next "news" coverage. If you think switching channels will enlighten you, it won't because the exact same stories are being played on every channel. The same in the papers and online. This is the laziest example one can ever see being presented to us as "news." No one is out investigating anything, researching anything, or digging into uncovering anything. They just read out the same script every single day, save for a few names or details. They are simply there to give us the illusion that we are being "informed and educated" when we are actually being misinformed and distracted from the truth.

The Real Purpose of the News

Aside from promoting products and marketing, what the news does is sell fear: fear of your neighbours, fear of every stranger, fear of going outside, fear of leaving the house, fear of driving your car, and fear of earthquakes. Why? Because fear is big business and sells. There are so many products like car alarms, house alarms, monitoring systems, guard dogs, extra insurance, fences, antitheft devices, extra lighting, and motion detectors. The more "stuff" you own, the more it has to be "protected."

The other thing fear does is keep us all alone and isolated from each other, in our little "protected personal space." Our "safe zone." If you are familiar with the term "divide and conquer," these are the ingredients required.

Keep people afraid and distrustful of each other. Keep to yourself. Don't interact with your neighbours, they might kill you. This is the "divide" part. When people are divided, they feel alone, vulnerable, and unsafe. This is how we are "conquered." Paralyzed from all that fear and distrust and distanced from others. Where is the sense of safety? From your security devices. Watch the "news" to make sure you know what is happening. The ones you pay to control us, conquer us through all that fear. It's paying off for the corporation because, once again, our loss is their gain. Whether it's paying for bottled water to those who poisoned it or paying for security for those who created the fear and paranoia, just keep watching the "news," and you will remain paralyzed in this prison.

In order to ensure we are terrified of everything and everyone, the "news" will make sure to keep feeding the fear-based "information," the information that is of no use to you, nor can you do anything about it, so it leaves you feeling helpless, hopeless, and apathetic. So why bother? It's all hopeless. Just get some pleasure from buying things for a temporary fix. Or people use drugs or alcohol.

Since cigarette ads were banned from TV commercials because of public health concerns with tobacco use, and because children were targeted, the industry had controls put on them. All you have to do is watch a movie on Netflix and other streaming services, and you will see people smoking like never before. The corporations are laughing all the way to the bank. To them, keeping kids and the public safe from tobacco, with the ad ban, was a failure, and they will not accept that. So, they have increased their campaign promoting cigarettes with "product placement."

An example might be personalities on the program (or in the background) drinking a particular beverage. Watch closely and note, most movies or series now have one or more main characters smoking. So, one way or the other, regardless of how dangerous or lethal a product is to you or your health, the corporations will find a way to lure you into buying or using it.

One has to search long and hard to find anything on hundreds of programs—TV, Netflix or any number of options—that is about something other than drugs, cartels, or trafficking. These shows always involve extreme violence. Or there are a plethora of crime shows, also usually about murder and solving crimes. Or there's some "supernatural force" killing or taking over someone's body. Then there are shows about missing, abducted people. I am horrified at what children are watching at home or at friends. Even the "news" is terrifying for children, and they are being traumatized by what they see and hear there. Yet parents allow them to watch that as well as terrifying, violence-filled shows or video games for "entertainment." How is this part of raising a healthy child and society? It's not. But it sure will keep us divided and afraid of each other. Recently, there seems to be a trend to introduce programs or shows on TV that glamorize hunting and guns. In fact, one is called *Gun Stories.* It glamorizes how they look like a thing of beauty, of value. We are not, as a mainstream, much into hunting and shooting, but with channels like The Outdoor Channel, survivalism and hunting are all being normalized and accepted. No doubt, once again, the axis of evil is working at selling products: lethal guns. The NRA is losing support in the

USA and looking for new markets for their bottom line, with politicians and media alongside.

The reason we have a better and safer society in Canada is that we are not a gun-enthusiastic nation. That makes the USA one of the worst, most violent places in the world. We must act immediately to prevent these programs and shows from being available 24/7, or once again, we, the people, will be victimized by mass shootings like in the USA, victims again of the axis of evil. Demand these programs be shut down to prevent acceptance and normalization of guns and killings. We need everyone in large numbers to protest this and nip it in the bud. This is how the axis of evil slowly, gradually, and subtly allows these destructive tools into our lives while profiting from violence and the killing of citizens. If you think we are distracted from saving the planet now, they will love it if we are so distracted with daily mass shootings, people will never be able to unite and fight for humanity or the planet. Don't let them get away with this. No guns and promoting of gun culture in Canada. It will be the end for hope or progress to make the world safer and better for all of us. Speak up. Act.

Combatting the Axis of Evil - Politicians are Not Working for You

How does taking the above steps help disempower the "axis of evil?" We, the masses, can be a very powerful force if we actually decided to unite with each other, our neighbours, and our communities. If millions or billions decided to fight for a healthy world and planet, a better future for our children, the "axis of evil" would actually be forced to confront the issues and listen to our anger, outrage, and demands.

They might actually have to expend time, energy, and the worst part of all, money. Having to spend money on fixing the problems they have created to make the air, water, and the planet clean and pristine again means they have to give up some of their profits (blood-money). They will only do it if forced to. Many of the politicians apparently think it is better to get bribes from these corporations than to fight for us, the people who pay the taxes whom they are supposed to protect and represent. So, they take the money and look the other way when the corporations poison the air and water, we all need to survive. Or they actively obstruct and cover up for the corporations to prevent the truth from coming out. And the final part of the well-oiled machinery in place is the media that will continue to give us the "news," which is a total diversion from the truth, is totally deceitful and full of bold lies. So, these three powerful systems are working for the protection of the corporate world while simultaneously destroying the real world that we live in. This is happening right under our noses while we "educate" ourselves with the "news," listen to the words from politicians, and the message that shopping is the answer or cure for all things. This is a system designed to destroy the quality of your life and that of your children in the worst possible way. And we are ignoring all of this because everyone is trapped into working, raising their children, paying their bills, and staying away from their "killer" neighbours.

What is the reality? What do we see and know? What we do "know" is in times of tragedy, our "murderous" neighbours are coming forward to help each other. Strangers bring food, blankets, help people out of their homes if there is a flood or an earthquake. The neighbours are there before any so-called services. Helping is their first thought and action. What do we "know" is there is "strength in numbers." "Divided we fall." "A house divided against itself it cannot stand." I am reminded of how often the Sikh community came forward on multiple occasions over my lifetime. Even when we were total strangers, they did so happily with a sense of a shared community bond. Not once did anyone ever ask or suggest we needed to pay back one penny. They gave generously to help as they always do.

The "axis of evil" knows this too. They don't want us to know. Or to remember it. They can't conquer us if they can't divide us. They do not want to stop destroying the planet or change the Ponzi scheme. And the only way they can try and prevent us from holding them to account, demand they stop their criminal behaviour, is to work together against us, the very people that give them their wealth. The very people that are profiting from us are the same ones destroying us and the planet. The more they destroy, the more trillions in profit they can make. Meanwhile, you and your children can't drink the water which was clean and free for billions of years. Children can't go out and play because of the poor air quality or because of the "killers" living next door. We become helpless and feel powerless.

Corporations continue to merge, becoming the one and only absolute rulers and controllers of us and the planet. Are these the forces that should be in charge of deciding your fate, the fate of your children, their future, and the planet? The planet with the wildlife or species that we cannot survive without? The forces that are cutting down every inch of the Amazon Forest, literally the lungs of the planet. Our lungs. Killing Indigenous people and exterminating all the species living there. This must be stopped. We need to stomp out our mutated culture and re-establish our relationship to the natural world—not money, not products. The natural world that we are dependent upon in the best possible way. It is what gives us life, water, air, and food. We only have to respect it and all the species we share the planet with. They are our partners in survival. They all work together to allow us to live and thrive. Corporations do not "own" the planet. The earth's air, water, soil, moon, and sun do not belong to any species, and the mutated ones are the last ones that should be "in charge or control" of any of it. We are the only ones out of billions of species over billions of years that have brought it to the brink of total devastation and destruction: we and the "axis of evil." We need to break away from this dangerous liaison and rejoin our biological partner: nature, our living home, our nurturer, and the giver of all the things we *need*.

We don't have to keep destroying ourselves and the future over *wants*. These are killing everything. It's time for a change. Time to go back to what worked for billions of years—tried, tested, and true—and will remain for billions of years.

It's time for a global movement, a revolution, to get the health, survival, and life of the planet out of the hands of the" axis of evil." This global movement to save the planet for our survival must make demands.

A CALL TO ACTION

Below is a practical list of solutions that humans can employ to turn things around. We must dismantle the "axis of evil."

End all Wars

There needs to be a global movement to end all wars. We can't keep dropping bombs on the planet or each other. The Earth is dying. People are dying. Wildlife is dying. The oceans are dying. Everything is being bombarded with bombs and millions of tons of toxins and poisons and garbage every day. They are literally blowing up the earth to pieces of wreckage. There is too much violence and suffering in everyone's life. Anyone living through a war or war zone has PTSD. The planet has become a war zone. We and the planet need peace. Look around. Where there is nature, there is peace and beauty. Where there are mutant humans, there is destruction and chaos. Our peace must be connected to protecting the earth. Too many places around the globe are being run by tyrants, war-mongering dictators, psychopaths and greed. Globally the "axis of evil" is on display. They must be removed—no more manufacturing and sales of war machinery.

Forgive all Debts

Since Covid-19 hit, everyone is broke. Let's start over with an equal slate. Too many countries are being exploited and stuck in extreme poverty because of unfair lending practices. If people can live in their own countries with resources without violence and war, they do not need to escape in the millions seeking refuge for themselves and their children.

Debts should also be forgiven since the impact of colonialism around the globe has exploited and destroyed peoples and their culture, pillaged riches, destabilized and prevented an equal playing field in terms of power and wealth. These effects continue to prevent financial success and an equal voice in the world. Since the actions of the colonizers cannot be erased, the debts must be. Restitution must be made to all those impacted by the devastation and violence of colonialism.

Every person who meets the threshold should receive a living wage. Since elected officials are not working to ensure fair access to opportunities jobs, wealth, and an economy that is sustainable, people should not have to suffer when they mismanage funds causing shortfalls, vulnerable to stock markets or other things not under our control. Everyone should have enough to meet their basic needs and this would provide more equity, security and allow people to contribute to society without being subject to homelessness because they cannot afford to pay the rent. There is plenty of wealth to do this, the wealthy need to start paying their share of taxes.

Reduce Population Growth

There needs to be a global movement to reduce human population growth and infinite development of land. The earth cannot sustain almost half a million babies per day. We must live within nature's blueprint. We must live in a sustainable way. The only way this can happen is to stop putting every inch of the planet under cultivation and development. We kill off all species and the planet, and we kill ourselves. We must protect the planet from the mass destruction of all life for the sole purpose of expanding the human population. It can't and won't work no matter how many lies we are told. Don't keep adding children to a life of extreme suffering, with things only getting worse for every generation. Children and teenagers need to be engaged and informed about the state of things so they can avoid all the "traps" being set for them as soon as they are born. Don't keep living on "autopilot," with our brains turned off. We have created more human suffering in every single way from starvation, human trafficking and the historic number of refugees seeking a safe place to live. They don't want to leave their countries, but they are fleeing war and atrocities, and they desire for their children to have a chance to survive.

Reduce Consumerism

Stop buying products and things you don't need. Don't get tricked into buying so-called necessities that have been free but for the corporations poisoning them. For example, when city water to our home may have been turned off short-term or even a few hours to correct an issue, we can drink tap water again. I never buy bottled water for my home. I, and most people I know, do the same. But many people, once they believe something has been "tainted," accept this as a permanent condition and that the tap water can never be ingested again. I am not referring to areas that have an absolute problem accessing clean water. But millions of us continue paying out billions of dollars every year for water. Even though we already pay for the water through our taxes, we just buy water instead of holding the officials accountable. In a case where a corporation has damaged the water source through chemicals and poisons, again, we, not the politicians, not the media, none hold them accountable. We just pull out the wallet and pay some more for something that had always been free to all on earth. Poisoning and killing us should not be profitable.

Stop production and buying of anything that is not biodegradable. There are many things already available that can be used that are cheap and not harmful to you, your children or the planet, for example, vinegar can be used as a cleaning product around the house. If you choose to have children, you must be willing to do the right thing. Stop using disposable diapers—demand "green" products.

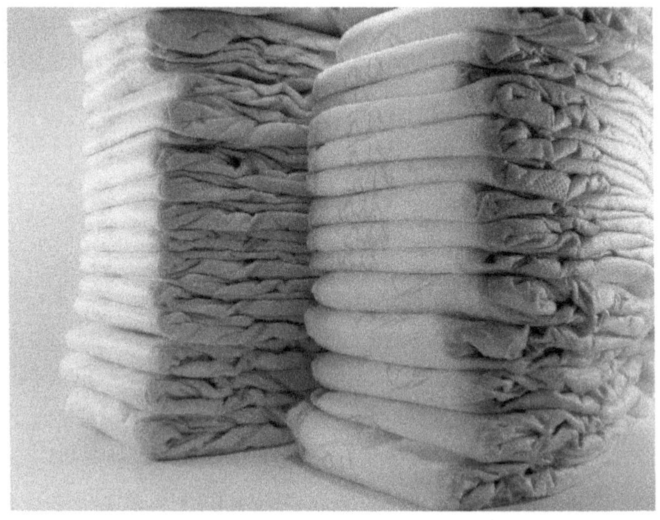

Disposable diapers.

Go to the stores and get a petition or signatures demanding cleaner, greener products. The more these are made on a massive level, the less they will cost. We must demand that environmental concerns be at the forefront of every decision. The industries must transition to genuine green goods, not fake ones that just advertise themselves as such. If it is harmful to the planet, it must be banned. We should not be purchasing and bringing into our homes or lives things that harm our children and their future. Stand up for your children and their right to a clean, safe planet. This needs to be your loudest voice. Your children need to hear this voice. We can't just be silent and look the other way. Your children are watching and listening to what you do and don't do. You are supposed to be their strongest advocates.

I don't have children, but I am fighting for them. For all children. For their future. So, they can live with the hope of having their basic needs for air, water, and food. Don't be quiet, in denial, complicit. We need to start shouting what we need for the sake of billions of children. Your children won't care about designer jeans after you are gone, and they are left to face the devastation. How will they know how to fight for their well-being and rights if the adults in their lives are not doing it now, showing them, modelling it? Stop buying your children out of guilt because you know what needs to be done, and it is not. The kids know it. Greta Thunberg knows it. As a young teenager, she is showing all parents, adults, and teens what we all should be doing. We cannot afford to be lazy or apathetic. We have to care; we have to bother to put in some effort. Even if it is just changing our personal choices in choosing green products or having smaller families, we all personally need to do what is within our reach or capacity to make things better. Don't let others get away with not caring. Call them on it if they use harmful things, or litter, or shop addictively. Push others to understand what is at stake—their own survival, the children's survival, and the capacity for the earth to sustain us. This is the only home we have; we must all be responsible for taking care and not causing harm.

Hold Elected Officials Accountable

We need to start holding elected officials accountable. They need to produce results each and every year in office. Let's push for laws that hold them responsible to actually do their job. In a case where they act in bad faith, corruptly, or do anything illegal, they should be held personally responsible, just like any of us would be if we acted in such a negligent or criminal way. They should not be allowed to take our money, then act *against* us. They should not be allowed to accept *any* money from a corporation or anything constituting a conflict of interest. If they do, they must be charged criminally and receive the appropriate sentence. The tight financial relationship between corporations, industries, and elected officials is a serious conflict of interest and must be severed. This would break the axis.

We can no longer let elected officials do everything in secret, behind closed doors, and of course, with no honest media coverage. Our tax money is being used in ways and in a manner, we never intended, and if it is not being used to benefit the citizens directly (and for the protection of the earth), it cannot be used without our knowledge or consensus.

The axis of evil survives because we allow it to. Millions of people need to start demanding more from their elected officials. Not allow them to be in those positions for decades or a lifetime while accomplishing nothing to protect the rights of people for a better world and better living conditions.

The rest of us have regular job evaluations and are put on notice when there are concerns. If they are not corrected, we can lose our job. If we commit crimes like embezzlement or sexual assault, we can be charged and held liable. There *must* be real consequences, criminal consequences, for elected officials. Things will never improve, and government waste, corruption, and lack of service to the people will continue. Only when people are personally accountable and punishable will they be compelled to start doing the right thing for people and the planet. We can't afford to pay people for decades with nothing to show for it. Only elected officials get away with this year after year. They seem to have no regrets, shame, or guilt for working against their own people. We can't allow them to get away with this anymore.

There is no time for all the delay tactics being used by them and the corporate world. They keep using courts to obstruct any fight by the people to hold them accountable. No one is on *our* side. We can't overlook this any longer. The "axis of evil" is against us. We and the earth must be on the same side.

Any system or environment that is secretive and anonymous is going to be subject to abuse. Just as on social media, unsuspecting people are deceived out of money or put in harm's way because they really don't know who that person is on the other end. The person who is running a scam can do so because of their anonymity. You don't know who they are, what they really look like, or where they live. In this same way, elected officials can scam us because we are in the dark about what they are doing on a day-to-day basis. How many hours do they actually work? What are they spending our money on? With whom are they in association or partnership? Which contracts for service are they approving based on nepotism or corruption? Many of the contracts' taxpayers are footing the bill for are extremely inflated costs being paid out to friends and family, with kickbacks or to help launder money for criminal enterprises. This is not how our tax money is supposed to be used. It is taking money from the collective community and giving it to individuals. I say enough. This system needs total dismantling.

Just as every household receives a monthly statement from their bank, with a detailed statement of credits and debits, the elected officials must be required to do the same. After all, it is the people's money paid through their taxes. It is not cumbersome and should be made available online every month. Every dollar should be accounted for every month. This way, everyone (regardless of position) will be much more diligent in ensuring they are efficient and not wasting funds. Particularly as government gets bigger (municipal, provincial, and federal), there is less accountability and transparency. This way, we, the people, will keep in check their spending, what is misused, such as using taxpayer dollars for expensive furniture or travel. And what was illegal, such as paying for things that are for their personal use, family or nepotism. This will keep in check chronic problems of unethical conflict of interests, shady partnerships, and deals. Even when this is discovered, the money is never returned to the taxpayer. If citizens are tired of hearing, there are "insufficient funds" for any of our basic needs (affordable shelter, health care, education, transition to green economies), we can only dispute and challenge this if/when we get a monthly statement, in real-time. If we can see the funds, where every dollar went, we will know exactly how much there is and how it has been spent. There must be total transparency and accountability. If there are repeat offenders not being responsible with taxpayer money, they need to be replaced.

There are a million examples of departments doing nothing.

Consumer protection is not protecting consumers.

Environmental Protection is not protecting the environment.

Fisheries and Oceans are not protecting fish or oceans.

Housing departments are not providing housing.

Food and Drug regulators are not regulating.

This is an infinite list. Why are we paying departments to provide us with services and protections when they do neither? Instead, they capitulate to the corporations. If this is going to continue to be the case, we should dismantle all these departments and have *one* department that deals with the agency that is creating all the problems for us and the planet: Corporations. Maybe we need one larger, powerful global agency whose sole purpose is to put corporations back to their rightful place and dedicate staff whose mandate is to prevent corporations from controlling every aspect of our life, disabling all the agencies from doing the job for people and planet. They need to prevent payments that create conflicts of interest, prevent them from becoming monopiles and stomping out everyone and everything in their path to destroying the planet. They need to be stopped from dumping waste, overdeveloping and destroying habitats and species. We need one agency whose sole purpose is to protect people and planet from the harmful effects of corporations on the world. The agencies and organizations that are actually doing the work of saving the planet are dependant on charitable donations from us, the ones already paying the government for these services. Since these dedicated people are already proving successful and competent, lets shut down the government departments that are failing and divert our taxpayer money directly to these organizations. We are already paying for services we don't get, and these organizations are actually doing the work and need funds. This should be a no brainer. Why should we pay for everything twice?

Locally, I believe it is important for citizens to have a say in how the "household" money is allocated. We are the "shareholders." We should benefit when there are profits since we pay the cost when there are losses. If people can see (as an example) in the statement that $300,000 was planned to be spent on fireworks by their city, but there is a lack of daycare or hospital beds, we can prevent this money from being spent on fireworks. Frankly, fireworks are costly, harmful to the planet, noisy, and harmful to animals. We can start making better, smarter choices on what we *need*, rather than what some official decided or wanted for a photo op for PR. Taxes should be beneficial directly to all taxpayers and the environment. Discretionary expenses should be done by consensus. Particularly when year after year there is always a shortfall for essential services. It must be transparent to ensure the safety, health, and well-being of the people, wildlife, and the environment. We all want clean air, water, and safe living conditions. We need to make sure the priorities are paid for before there is spending on anything that might be "frivolous" or unnecessary. A huge document with 100,000 pages listing the budget is not going to be read by the masses, and they know it. That is why it is done that way. No, send us the running tab online available in real-time. I should be able to look at it anytime I want or need to look at or question anything. I want to know where they plan to spend every dollar *before* it's spent. Too late, then. I should be able to see it by country, province, and municipality, at any time. Enough wasting our money and betraying us while at the same time engaging in criminal activity. Only when they are forced to expose transactions and spend transparently will all citizens having real-time access. Let's see how far the money will go to basic necessities once that happens, like healthcare, housing, education, and environmental protection. It can all be afforded once citizens have access to and input into our taxpayer funds. No more secret deals with the "axis of evil." The people should have much more direct input into exactly where the money goes and how much. We will be able to have the previous year's spending and monitor whether the new allotments seem reasonable or they way off and suspicious. The private party at the expense of people and planet is over. Our existence and future of the planet is at risk. We can't afford to let irresponsible, reckless people be in charge of the money and how it is spent.

Similarly, on the federal level, I do not want my taxpayer money going towards funding any wars. Nor to give tax breaks or subsidies to corporations. They need to have accountability to ensure money is being spent to directly help the planet and people. Wars don't do that. Corporations don't do that. I don't want my tax money to go to people or organizations that are poisoning me and future generations. If they are not willing to provide this level of transparency, then they do not get voted in. We have to get our voice and power back. *Corporations have used their wealth and power to obtain the legal status* ***of a living person.***

Do most people know corporations gained the legal status of being "a real person?" No, the "axis of evil" won't mention that. Who allowed this to happen, to be approved? Did the public vote on this? Did local politicians warn the citizens of this and what the implications would be to the economy, people, or the planet?

According the World Trade Organization one of their rules is: **"The Parties to this Agreement [recognize] that their relations in the field of trade and economic endeavour should be conducted with a view to raising standards of living, ensuring full employment and a large and steadily growing volume of real income and effective demand, and expanding the production of and trade in goods and services, while allowing for the optimal use of the world's resources in accordance with the objective of sustainable development, seeking both to protect and preserve the environment and to enhance the means for doing so in a manner consistent with their respective needs and concerns at different levels of economic development ..."**

It seems as though the part that has to do with protecting the environment is not being given the importance it should, but it is focused more on exploiting the earths resources as pure commodities to be extracted for trade and profit. This approach needs to be replaced with the protection of people and planet first and the other objectives as secondary. What will the WTO stand for once the earths resources have been depleted? Our so-called taxpayer-funded officials representing their states or countries allowed all his to happen, speaking for billions and not giving us any thought or voice.

Corporations should not be "designated a person." They are using this to gain so-called rights and privileges and protections afforded to people, real people, humans. In the commercial world, they, with their trillion-dollar companies, want to be treated as a "regular person" like you and me! This status allows them to make large donations (bribes) to political parties just as a person is allowed to. This allows this axis of evil to exist and destroy. This allows politicians to accept hundreds of millions of dollars to represent the corporations and their interest and protection, not the people or planet. That is why nothing is done to help people and planet year after year. This "person" is allowed to evade paying taxes back to the people and planet it destroys with the full support of elected officials. As a result, they have accelerated their destruction of life and the planet on a bigger scale and increased their profits astronomically. A nonliving entity, a corporation, is being treated as human, while actual living beings on the planet have been turned into inanimate objects, products to use, destroy, and profit from. This is beyond incredible, criminal and unjust. It is an absurd abuse to designate one of the axes of evil, "a person." They cannot be poisoned or be killed. The corporation does not have living offspring or living, breathing future generations. This designation must be repealed. It must not be allowed to retain this absurd designation. Period.

The corporation should not be able to play this game of hypocrisy. If they are designated "a person" with all the rights, privileges, and protections afforded a person, then using this designation, so should they, as "a person" be responsible, held accountable, and be punishable as any other person. If a person poisons one person or causes injury or death to another, including if a person dumped poison in the local stream, they can be charged criminally and be incarcerated. The more severe the crime, the more severe the punishment. There is no statute of limitations on murder and premediated crimes resulting in death. This "person" needs to be held accountable. Not given financial penalty since that is no deterrent and never will be, because they pay the fines and continue committing crimes against humanity and the planet. The CEO needs to be personally held responsible, and if their excuse is "they are accountable to their shareholders," perhaps the shareholders can be held responsible as co-conspirators and also face prosecution. This could fall under "organized" crime and racketeering as well. Enough abuse of people and planet while they all laugh to the bank!

They are acting in concert to commit crimes against humanity and the planet for their own financial interest. A "person" is not allowed to do this and escape criminal prosecution. Neither should a powerful corporation worth billions, and trillions hide behind their "personhood." Animals need to be designated the same rights as a person. Not a nonliving entity. It is time to launch a global criminal and civil case against the "axis of evil" for allowing this to occur while keeping billions in the dark. How many billions did these secret handshake dealmakers get paid by the richest, most powerful "person" in the universe? All so they can accelerate the destruction of humanity and the planet that is now on the brink of total collapse and extinction. Where is the people's legal dream team to reverse this? This must be fought in the courts, and whatever bodies allowed this to happen should be brought to justice. All need to be held personally responsible. All people, including the corporate entity masquerading as a "person."

Demand Truth in News

Demand "news." Tell those reading an identical script every day, that the "gig is up." You will no longer watch it until they actually start telling the truth about what is happening in the world. Investigate and report actual factual information that can help your life and future generations be better. Have TV blackout days. Don't watch the "news'" ads and commercials. This is the main purpose of TV. Not to report the news but to market and sell products to you. Be selective until you find stations, programs, and podcasts that speak the truth. There are many options. Just say no to lies and manipulation. Public TV is very inexpensive by donation. Better programs that are not part of the "axis of evil."

Unplug and Engage

Unplug yourself and unplug the kids. Start spending quality time around dinner tables every day if you are not. Talk about the important things your children may have anxieties about. Many of them may not feel they have permission to bring up issues about global warming or how their lives might be when you are no longer around. They need to be informed and be active, so they don't remain apathetic and irresponsible like their previous generation (us and our parents). Stop shopping and playing on devices and start engaging. Have shopping blackouts like TV and device blackouts. Maybe a day a week will turn into a week at a time. That helps ease out of bad habits.

If Greta can get on the world stage to tackle a critical issue to help all of us, millions more young people better start putting together ways they can join in or start their own organizations. Teenagers can become great leaders and confront elected officials, and they are the future purchasing powers, so they can start demanding clean products and demand the corporations clean up the mess they have created. Don't buy their products if they don't show actual evidence that can be seen and measured, such as repairing the damage and destruction to the planet and water systems. Remove from the ocean's debris, plastics, and harmful substances destroying marine life. This applies to everything on the planet. No more profiting from poisoning people and planet. Get schools involved. Don't allow corporations to fund things in exchange for them feeding you junk food or unhealthy food. These corporations should be providing healthy foods and products for free as some restitution for all the harm they have done to the planet. They should be providing the planet restitution. They should not be getting tax breaks and subsidies from the government (you and me) so they can increase their profit, not put any money back in taxes to the people and get to make money from killing us.

Unite

The one advantage of media and social media is that it can take a movement to become global in a day. If we designate a day to begin this movement for world peace and the protection of people and planet, it can be like a wildfire in real-time. We saw it happen recently with Black Lives Matter after the killing of George Floyd. It literally went around the globe, and millions around the world marched in the streets in support of Black Lives Matter. This made elected officials and corporations take notice. CEOs gave their position to a black person. A US presidential candidate withdrew during this time to not run against a black candidate. Companies changed their icons and logos that were considered racially insensitive. We need to unite as humans. Mass peaceful protests work.

One voice for one planet. I think this is the time. More people are ready than ever before. We can't let this chance be missed. It may be our last. Our kids are waiting, and they will follow. Get block eco-parties and projects. Come together in small groups and join them to become larger groups. It needs coordination to gain in numbers and strength. This is a higher purpose that humanity can share and accomplish. Get our humanness back. Become the humane people we are meant to be, not what we have allowed others to make us. Indigenous people are living it; every species is living it. We just have to join them. We won't be alone. There will be billions of us doing it together. What should we call this movement? One Planet One People?

<u>Local Ideas for a Better Community.</u>

Stop engaging in violent video games and movies. Violence is leading to an increase in anxiety in kids.

Read more.

Learn how other kids and people live in different parts of the world. Make a connection.

Raise funds or donations to give to those in need. Instead of buying another item you don't need, donate to help a cause.

Do things like plant trees and edible gardens, for yourself and your neighbours.

Arrange for Co-op equipment in your local area or block so everybody does not have to buy lawnmowers, shovels, games, etc. Maybe a church can be used for this.

Use manual lawnmowers. They are better for health and the environment.

Have a neighbourhood BBQ or potluck once a month or so, where everyone can get to know each other.

Make ethical financial investments.

Don't use pesticides.

Welcome new neighbours like we used to.

Dog sit for each other.

List a new thing that you got from the planet every day (food, water, clothing).

Offer to tutor a kid.

Help someone learn to play a sport.

Teach a child a musical instrument. Lots of people are at home or retired that would like someone to ask. They need to feel needed.

Visit elderly people in a home or facility and with a pet, if allowed. They love babies and children too. Maybe sing or play a game. Ask them about their life and history.

Don't allow others to bully.

Telling the truth is not snitching.

Learn new words.

Designate days with no devices or technology.

Include people, and kids; don't exclude others.

Play puzzles and games to improve skills with friends and family. Ask family what games they played with no technology.

Help each other share.

Rent a sheep for trimming a lawn as an example of cutting pollution (noise or otherwise). Get creative.

Eat less meat and high-sugar foods. Let's take care of our bodies and mind.

Make cookies with grandparents. Learn how to cook.

Don't accept or tolerate kids or people being mean to others or animals.

Help bring back bees and birds.

Don't create habits in little children that are not healthy for them or the planet.

Stop money laundering in real estate and government contracts.

Build everything sustainable.

Support non-fossil fuel transportation. Use a bike or electric car.

Improve soundproofing for condos and townhomes. It is unhealthy to be subjected to multiple sources of noise night and day. Many move only to be in the same situation. Where is the protection for people, not businesses? They get to reduce building costs at the buyer's expense.

Reduce development—demand more wild areas.

Be grateful for an education. Try hard and ask for help if needed. Change and improve teaching methods or curriculum that is effective and more individual to how people learn.

A global response is required to get land back from the drug cartels and corporations who are preventing locals from growing the food needed. They cannot eat poppy or coca leaves or coffee beans. Go back to local production for local use.

Make it illegal to buy and sell Earth's creations that every living thing needs to survive—water, air, trees, and soil.

No commodification of living things. Nature is not a product.

Go back to local people using only the minimum of nature's resources within their area.

Force or shut down so-called departments that are supposed to protect citizens and the environment that are taking money and doing nothing. Water protection? Why are people paying for?

Consumer protection? Why are we buying new faulty products that break down all the time? Why are "consumers" not protected from corporations that sell these substandard products?

It should be illegal to pay for drinking water. If the corporation pollutes it, they must immediately pay the cost to repair it and provide water to affected people and the environment at their expense.

Adopt a pet from a rescue shelter.

Get your pet spayed or neutered.

Make sure your vet respects the oath they take to do no harm. That they do not do painful procedures that have no medical basis (like docking ears, tails, and removing claws). Always treat animals with respect.

Help each other at home with chores.

Don't hit, yell, or swear in the home or to others. Be respectful towards each other.

Create a new sustainable economy with alternatives beyond currency. Too many people are stealing or misappropriating money and destroying the planet due to greed.

Clean up the neighbourhood streets.

Walk someone's dog.

Walk each other's kids to school. Lots of people want to contribute.

Help shovel snow and leaves for people who need help.

Play with friends.

Parents, get fit with your kids. Go for a walk in the park or a hike together. Cook at home. Learn recipes from Mom, Dad, and Grandparents before they are gone.

Have discussion times for family and with neighbours. Talk about how to make things better for each other.

Think about how to make the planet better.

Encourage smaller families.

Get involved and vote the right people in.

Demand clean water. We should not have to pay for this. We already pay for city services.

Save money.

Stop collecting. It is buying unnecessary things.

Promote acceptance, not hate.

Respect all living things.

If you don't want to encounter animals in the wild in in the water, don't go there. They have no choice, they live there, in their home. You may cause the animal to be killed if a animal is protecting territory

Plants and insects, and the planet nurture us and help keep us alive. Protect them.

Discourage people from doing wrong things like littering and lighting fires.

Help conserve and protect species in our areas, too, like bears, coyotes, eagles, and other birds. Plant foods they can eat and protect their area, so they don't have to come into the high-density areas for food to scavenge.

Don't let the media off the hook when they "report" animals are "attacking" us. They are not. They are only trying to live. Call or write to them to inform them.

Stop eating anything that is threatened. If any source is sparse or threatened, do not eat it. Leave it for the species that have no other food to eat. We can eat anything and everything and store food.

Don't buy animal cruelty products. Push for cruelty-free products. Demand a ban on using animals in cruel experiments.

Demand natural products and ban any substance or product harmful to the planet.

Stop using disposable products of every kind—especially diapers and feminine products.

Try hard not to waste food. Share rather than throw away. Lots of animal shelters can use food scraps.

Don't upgrade every device every time.

Donate clothes, shoes, eyeglasses, and toys.

Tell others if something is helping the community so they can do it too.

Parents and children need to make sure all are recycling, not throwing everything in the garbage.

People who do the right thing for the community and planet (like recycling, using fewer resources, keeping the city and their neighborhood clean) should get a tax rebate to encourage others to do the same.

Come up with your own list and share it with others.

Get the media to focus on these types of ideas.

So, there is a plan. There is hope. There is a better future. Now we are at what began as the primary reason for writing this book. I actually had not intended to write anything else. Just a book of maxims, truths if you will. But it occurred to me that no one knows me. I am not famous like Oprah that people will just want to run out and read my "truths." So, it occurred to me to say something about how I became me. I did this as minimally as possible to get to the compass. But I realized I am probably never going to write anything again. I am a late bloomer in a lot of things. Once I had included my mentors and talked about *Ishmael* and how it changed my life, I ignited that passion, the activist in me. How can I not use this chance to speak about the most important cause to me, the one I am fiercely passionate about: protecting the planet and allowing nature to sustain life for generations to come. And how we can help ourselves in the process? That has now got me to the Compass.

THE COMPASS

Maxims For Living While Human

THE COMPASS

Reflect upon and clearly define your values and principles.

Never violate your principles or allow others to.

Values and principles provide not only your path but also your boundaries.

What you would not do, nor allow others to. Without these, it would be like turning up for a new job with no job description. What you are expected to do, and what are the consequences for not doing them.

If you value honesty, a principle might be, "never lie." This identifies what you should expect from yourself and others. The more of them you define, the clearer your path will be.

Your principles will always guide you to the right path.

When in doubt, refer to your principles.

Make every decision and take every action consciously. Think it through.

Living by one's principles passes the test of time, and they are increasingly validated and confirmed.

Change your friends, not your principles. Compromising them is the quickest way to get lost and make wrong decisions.

The first puzzle in life we need to solve is ourselves. Analyze yourself fully. Evaluate yourself. Who are you, what do you stand for, what are you willing to do or not do? Only then can you live consciously.

Actions reveal what words conceal.

What is it that you would never want to be? Then why would you become that for someone else?

Beware of the person who is in "pursuit" of you. It implies you have reason to run.

Never assume someone you trust would never allow a dangerous person into your life. They may be unaware or lack the principles and boundaries to really know that person. There are many people, especially women, who were seriously harmed after being introduced by a close friend. Do not just allow this person into your private life without finding out for yourself who they really are. You will be relieved you did.

It is important your friends know to never give your personal information to anyone (phone or workplace). Even if they think it would be ok. That is for you to decide. Once your safe place is threatened, there is no easy way to make it safe again, especially if you have dependent children or loved ones. It is easier to change an email or phone than your home or place of work.

Do not allow others to violate your space. If they turn up at your home without calling despite being told, that is a red flag they lack respect and appropriate boundaries. Stop it at the first occurrence.

Do not make assumptions about a person based on appearance or position. Many people have trusted someone because they were "a church going person" or they had a certain job. This is irrelevant and should not be a factor in evaluating if they are appropriate. Use your principles, not the image.

The more someone pushes to get personal or intimate before you are comfortable, the further away they need to remain. This is a red flag. If they respect you, they will respect your boundaries.

Never cover (or look the other way) for anyone if they do something criminal or corrupt. You will have compromised your principles and placed yourself at risk to forever be a co-conspirator.

Never be silent if you witness abuse or maltreatment of any kind, regardless of your relationship with the abuser or victim. You might save a life and have a clear conscience.

There is nothing worse than regretting one did not do enough to help a person or animal in need.

If someone is angered or decides to sever contact because you did what was right, it is worth this cost. If they realize this, they will make amends. Either way, you are validated. Remember, change your friends, not your principles.

The consequences for telling the truth should not be the basis for it.

Never look the other way in your professional or personal life. It will haunt you and entrap you.

Successfully navigating life is only possible if you are comfortable being in it with yourself.

Once you live authentically, truthfully, and based on your principles, you will be able to recognize if others do.

It is easy to give a blank cheque you know can never be cashed.

Superficial people and conversations are of no interest to me.

As a teenager, I was keenly aware that I did not think or feel like my peers. Most went on to marriage and children. As time went on, many were either divorced or in their second or third marriage. As time went on, my choices became increasingly validated. I struggled to go against the mainstream at first but found happiness and fulfillment. Many others followed the path of least resistance and did not.

Do not make decisions based on fear. Fear is best used as a tool for survival when it is rooted in intuition and an immediate threat, not living in your mind.

Poor people are called insane while rich people are called eccentric.

The worst mental illness is the one people don't know they have.

The danger of those with delusions are they do not know of their delusions.

The Dali Lama has no need to refer to himself as a spiritual leader. Others do that because it is observed in his actions and in the love and generosity he emits.

Spirituality is never about the self or ego.

Anyone who feels compelled to proclaim themselves to be the only true spiritual leader are using empty words to convince others they should be believed or followed. This is the trait of a cult leader not a true spiritual being. Beware of the words used to deceive.

Have a tough mind but a soft heart.

A truth is still a truth, even if it is harsh.

Learn to trust and listen to your instinct, and do not override it with intellect. Intellect is for thinking; instinct is knowing.

People ask, "How do you know you are genuinely happy?" My response is, "It's like being in love, you just know."

Happiness cannot be learned, only discovered and felt.

When uncertainty creeps in, refer to your principles.

Always tell the truth, and you might be believed; tell a lie once, and you never will be.

Know the difference between information and wisdom; the first is readily available the latter must be actively sought.

I describe "mainstream" as a fast-moving body of masses that often take you where you did not need to go. Resist this powerful stream.

The "mainstream" becomes the default path when people have not self-reflected and defined their principles or boundaries.

Be confident with your beliefs and actions, even if they challenge the mainstream paradigm, as yours are based on your principles. Realize that in doing so, many may find your beliefs disconcerting, but these are usually people you do not need in your life.

Everyone does not have a right to be in my life. When based on principles, one discovers they have a smaller but more meaningful circle of people in their lives.

Being spiritual never means accepting others unconditionally. Being kind and loving should never be permission for others to abuse or treat one badly. Spirituality includes respecting and loving yourself first.

When you live by your truths and principles, you will find that healthy relationships are always respectful of who you are as a person.

The minute one is born, society begins to impose rules, obligations, and expectations that can imprison one for the rest of one's life.

Living a truly free life involves carefully dodging "traps" set for you: the education trap, the job trap, the money trap, the marriage trap, and the baby trap. Masses have unknowingly and happily jumped into these traps to discover themselves enslaved in a life they never envisioned nor desired.

Formal education is not preventing society from creating pathological individuals and behaviours. All the "experts," and the emphasis on "family values" are not preventing this. We forever update manuals, policies, and add offences to the criminal code to prosecute. Great legal and sociological thinkers of our time are not giving us ways to prevent this. Mass incarceration, the death penalty, and the so-called "deterrents" are not preventing this. The answer and solutions get further away when we individually and collectively detour from values and principles needed as our compass for living. Each of us must remain solid in our foundation of principles and not allow others to violate them. Each value or principle compromised leads to more of the same. Hence, the world we have created and passively accepted.

Children and youth need to learn skills to live as better humans while nurturing each other and the planet.

Important life choices should be made with reflection and honest discussion, not by accident.

The more space and freedom you give another, the less they feel the need for it.

People should always have the right to choose their destiny. Forcing someone to give up their needs, passions, or future can never result in a mutually happy or fulfilling relationship in the long term.

Our capacity for love and intimacy should be encouraged, not restricted.

When people use projection, they give clues about what they want.

Listen to the behaviour of others.

I am comfortable being called an iconoclast.

A gift should be given freely rather than on a socially dictated occasion.

When one is in control of their life, one does not want to control others.

Those who do not have a true sense of inner power are threatened by those who do.

Those who give up freedom for security get neither (unknown author).

A true sense of security lies within us and between our ears; therefore, it can never be threatened.

Our family members are not always people that offer us the wisdom that we require. They sometimes teach us that which one should not do or become. This is sometimes more important.

Question what others call your duty.

Needs should be respected, not imposed.

Be realistic without cynicism and optimistic without delusion.

True happiness and spirituality are a state of mind that is only achieved through life's experiences rather than through formal learning.

Spirituality is rooted in the simplest of experiences; truths are never complex and are easy to understand and easy to follow.

Always choose simplicity in life. Don't complicate your life or relationships.

Truths are universal and not subject to place or time, or age.

Spirituality is not related to or dependent upon religious dogma. It is, however, related to one's capacity to feel deep emotional intimacy and compassion with all living things.

Despite popular belief, people can remain single, have no children, and live happy, fulfilled lives.

A person who wants to lead must be willing to maintain their truth in the face of opposition.

Giving with pure joy is spiritual. Giving out of guilt is not.

After someone dies, all you have left are memories. Live in such a way when they are alive that your memories will be positive.

Count your blessings and hope you can count that high.

Differentiate wants from needs, and we find we have everything we need. Enjoy your wants but never confuse them for needs.

Do not confuse struggling with suffering. All species struggle to survive.

The world is created the same for everyone, but it is not experienced that way.

Being equal should not mean that women need to be more like men.

Guilt can become a life sentence.

Free yourself. No one else will.

Many die fighting for freedom, yet others give it away easily, allowing themselves to become captives.

Take a big risk and be yourself. When we have no fear that others can judge us, we no longer need to protect our deepest thoughts, emotions, and feelings.

The joy of loving is equal to the pain of loss.

There can never be too much laughter.

Dance like no one's watching because no one is.

Singing in the car with my dog makes the drive much more enjoyable for both of us.

Living things can never be owned.

Friends can be bought, but trust and love cannot.

Not all my significant relationships are with humans.

My furry friends never doubt my love or intentions.

Tension is unique to humans; I have never felt it in an elevator with any other species.

Loneliness does not exist once we realize we are a small part of the whole universe and that we share the planet with many species. Remember to make this connection. If you are not in a "relationship," remember, you are not alone.

Stop, wait, reflect; just be. Do not rush.

It is ultimately better to do something good than to just be good at doing something.

Do the right thing, even if it displeases others.

Be generous with warmth and affection; it has amazing healing powers.

If you would not do it if others were watching, then do not do it when they are not.

There is no possession worth giving up one's sense of peace for.

Many people in society seem to be living on "auto-pilot" and dangerously close to a crash.

Those who value money more than friends will have more money than friends.

Adventure is where you are. Misery is where you are.

The hunger for consumerism is insatiable. The only way for it to subside is to feed your inner self.

Music is the language for our soul. It can promote a feeling of spirituality, as can a deep intimacy with another.

Do not assume what everyone is saying is rational or sane. In fact, there is ample evidence that much of human behaviour is neither rational nor sane.

Doing nothing sometimes does something, doing something sometimes does nothing, and saying nothing sometimes says a lot.

The more you know, the more you know you do not know. This much I do know.

Humans like to believe there is a heaven above because we have turned Earth into hell.

Most great world leaders were not politicians.

Dysfunction and pathology have become the norm.

"Conducting a survey"—a tactic used to delay action.

The greatest mystery yet to be solved is explaining human self-destructiveness.

"Currency"—a tool used to create class distinctions.

Money cannot solve most of our problems.

"Species centric"—our inability to value anything not human

"Greed"—a pathological condition leading to the destruction of the planet.

Being who you are is living with courage, being like everyone else is not.

For every problem, there is a solution. It seems for every solution there is a problem.

Much of what we are taught are myths. Questioning them results in hostility and alienation from those who teach them.

Greed is the worst of all diseases.

People become enraged for petty things while being deaf and blind to the most critical issues.

The greatest love is the ability to let go; it is never easy but always right.

To learn the answers, we must first ask the questions.

Catchy phrases have replaced personal reflection and values.

Human needs are universal, wants are not.

Humans take simple things and make them complicated.

Think about the millions of tasks and activities that humans "have to do," on a daily basis throughout their lifetime to "live" that no other species does or must. Why are we so busy doing things that do not help us with living?

People can give themselves the illusion that they have lots of "friends" and are well "liked," but many do not exist in their real lives.

Laws and contracts are written in such a way that we pay lawyers to understand them. Laws applicable to all should be accessible and easy to understand. Laws, in fact, are not the same as truths.

Every year we face more difficulties in living and raising healthy, functioning individuals and communities than the year before. It is time to make the obvious conclusion that what we are teaching is not working.

If it does not work, stop doing it. Yet every year, we only do more of it.

We only value that which has a human imprint.

Many people spend thousands or even millions of dollars on a painting of an animal, but they will not donate a single penny to preserve the living one.

Icons and logos have become today's badges of honour.

Our rage is misplaced. People readily accept the destruction of the planet but act out of rage over a parking spot.

People from wealthy countries like to play being "poor," spending thousands on designer clothes that are tattered and torn. This does not make a person look humble, nor does it allow them to identify with a person living in poverty. Instead, it emphasizes the vast differences between the haves and have nots. No person living in poverty chooses to wear tattered clothes and rightly question why those with means would. It is more offensive.

Similarly, people love to watch "reality" shows like *Survivor,* where people pretend to struggle to survive. Everyone knows they will survive and get paid handsomely for it. All the while paying no attention to the actual reality of real people struggling to survive. Most of them don't.

Climb a mountain instead of the corporate ladder.

If it is harmful to the planet, it should be illegal.

If everyone is doing it, it is usually wrong.

Experiments for human benefit are being done on those who do not benefit.

Barring medical, nutritional needs, those who are particular about what they eat are simply not sufficiently hungry.

What is religion doing for the planet?

We are born free and spend the rest of our life imprisoning ourselves.

Life is a gift we are given; experience is a gift we must give ourselves.

Something is true until it no longer is.

When humans achieve something, it is called intelligence. When other species do, we call it instinct.

An animal or organism is able to replicate by camouflaging its surroundings to exact precision. That is keen observation and intelligence.

Notice how leaves reveal their most brilliant colours at the end of their cycle.

The most invasive species on the planet is the human.

"Kill it" seems to be our most common response.

Human's only predator is themselves.

I want to hear the beautiful song and harmony of birds, not the deafening sounds of human existence.

Noise pollution has become as damaging as other forms. And not just to humans.

There is always proof of truth. Faith may be a comfort, but it is not proof.

People would rather continue maintaining and fabricating lies and fantasies rather than admit they do not have the answer and have lied all along.

If you cannot answer your child's questions honestly when asked, what are you teaching them?

People create lies and myths when they have discomfort with the truth.

Many adults and parents delude themselves that they are protecting a child by telling them myths or fables. Why diminish nature by inventing myths?

Children have a powerful ability to sense danger. Lies are a representation of danger. People in a position of trust become figures of that danger. No authentic relationship can be possible without truth and trust.

In nature, I may feel a sense of danger if I face an animal that can harm me. But I know that it is because of a need for survival. Not out of hatred or anger. I do not continue feeling the sense of danger when I am no longer in that situation. With humans, the danger is powerful and far more threatening because it is unnatural, not rooted in a need to survive. I may continue to sense the threat, even though I am no longer in the presence of the danger. This seems to be unique between humans and should not be ignored.

Being uncompromising of our boundaries and principles are tools that can help protect us from threats posed by other humans.

Animals and infants can sense security and love. Many humans have lost that ability because their love, trust, or security was betrayed.

All young children seem to have natural rhythm. By adulthood, many have lost it. Natural joys and abilities are lost, but why?

Corporations and politicians are quite content to encourage more consumption and more debt. This keeps the masses trapped, with little capacity to reflect, resist, or create change. For positive change to happen, people need freedom from traps. Being stuck in the various traps makes this is near impossible.

THE PLANET

We need a global peace movement. Social and ecological justice depends on ending all wars. Wars create chronic human suffering and are destroying all life on the planet. We must stop dropping bombs on our home, Earth.

Money can no longer be the primary decider in family planning. The planet's capacity and human suffering must be a significant consideration.

Why do humans consider themselves to be superior to other species? All other species do only that which promotes their survival and that of their offspring. If humans are so intelligent, why are we the only species that struggles to promote our own survival and that of the planet?

Evolution always promotes strategies and behaviour to maximize survival. Where is the biological evidence that we are evolving in this manner?

Every species has survived and thrived with only that which is provided by nature—all but one, humans. Yet, our needs are the very same that the earth provides to all others.

No other species on this planet is at war with anyone, self-destructive, or incarcerated, except when we put them in captivity. None die by suicide, murder, or torture for the sole purpose of doing so.

Almost no species on the planet practices monogamy since nature promotes biodiversity. Humans are at best, serial monogamists.

Corporations are not alone in viewing humans as a commodity. In fact, many of us view each other in the same way, whether consciously or not. An abusive man may see a women's vulnerability as a commodity to exploit. A person may view someone's abject poverty as a commodity whose labour can be exploited. Children are often viewed as commodities subject to the fate of those in charge of them. In fact, humans are responsible for the illegal trade and trafficking of everything on the planet since it is viewed as a commodity, property to be owned. We use terms like "my" wife, children, dog, plants.

Society uses terms like "our" oceans, fish, water, trees, mountains, and in fact, these elements are used as examples of commodities in the dictionary. These are neither commodities nor personal property belonging to humans. Our sense of grandiosity is that we believe we "own" the most precious life-giving properties that belong to the earth. This sense of ownership justifies buying, selling, controlling, and destroying as if there are no other species on the planet.

Human and child trafficking is illegal since it blatantly makes humans a commodity. We find this aberrant. In the dictionary, traffickers are described as "using force, fraud, or coercion to lure their victims and force them into labour or commercial exploitation." Is this definition not precisely what humans are doing to every species on this planet? What we do to the planet and most animals should be referred to as trafficking and should also be illegal and criminally prosecuted.

It is time to create an international court to prosecute "crimes against the planet." Humans in this regard are the sole perpetrators of these atrocities.

If humans do to each other, what we do to other species (torture, hold hostage in bondage or captivity), we are diagnosed and labelled as sociopaths, psychopaths, and evil monsters. These people are locked away to protect society. Why do we consider it acceptable to inflict this on other living beings, holding them and the planet hostage and in human captivity?

There are virtually few problems that cannot be solved by having fewer humans on the planet.

Environmental organizations have generally ignored putting human overpopulation as the primary cause for all environmental problems. Nothing can be saved if we continue to add more humans to the planet.

Every year, there are discussions on how to fund more schools, more police, more hospitals, more roads, etc. Not one person has the leadership or good conscience to talk about sustainable family planning. The current approach is unsustainable and is about to collapse.

A mentor taught me that when people pressured her to have a child, she always replied, "We are waiting for a people shortage."

I see other species in what we call a "Zen-like state" or "in the moment" naturally, and humans rarely are.

Humans are the only species that create non-biodegradable waste.

Recycle, reuse, and reduce are not human concepts and have been operating in nature since the beginning of time.

Are you doing things within your means to care for your only home, the earth?

No one would knowingly allow their children to inherit a home poisoned with toxic waste or about to collapse, yet that is what we are doing by destroying the planet.

One's greatest investments should be in future generations by protecting the earth.

Procreating does not give one immortality. One is still dead. Immortality exists in the longevity of the planet.

At some point, we declared war on the planet. It is time for a truce. Nature must win for all of us to.

Species do complex things and make them simple. We take simple things and make them complicated.

Species evolve collectively, while humans seem too individually.

Some of the people I have met caused me to question Darwin's theory of evolution. Other species have not.

Be humbled by remembering that human intelligence is rooted in our observations and understanding of the natural world. The geometry of a spiderweb and the concept and the design for flight are examples of this.

Learn from nature—our greatest teacher.

More evidence is becoming available that all life on the planet is based on mathematical formulas that every species follows. These formulas are not happening by chance. They maximize the survival of the species.

Nature always maximizes output with the least amount of input. It only uses the minimum amount of energy to achieve its objective. Nature causes no harm to the survival of other species and produce no "waste" or garbage. Their waste is always biodegradable and, in fact, usually food for another.

Nature benefits all. Each member of each species is an equal shareholder.

A flower has a simple existence and yet brings tremendous beauty and joy to the world. So can we.

Living as any gender has its liabilities and benefits. Women always have the default role of life-givers and nurtures. However, it is not necessary to give birth to be a life-giver and nurturer. The earth is full of children and many species who need nurturing to survive. Each of us can give love, care, and nurturing to all life on this planet.

A spider's web is a display of beautiful, complex geometry. It is seemingly invisible, can tear easily if touched, yet can withstand a downpour of rain and heavy winds, all the while trapping the spider's food. That is some amazing engineering. See nature's intelligence.

Everything created by nature, regardless of species, is beautiful, symmetrical, artistic, and functional. All done in total silence. Nature does not create any form of pollution.

The most restful sleep I ever had, was falling asleep and waking up to the gentle sound of the waves.

What will money buy us when we cannot breathe the air?

We need Mother Earth; she does not need us.

Name one species on the planet that is able or allowed to expand infinitely without natural checks and balances. None except one. We are the only ones who do so, but nature must and will create a balance even with our rebellion and resistance.

Daniel Quinn, author of *Ishmael*, pointed to laws that exist within the biological community of life. These, Quinn refers to as the "peacekeeping laws" that all but humans follow. Humans' failure to recognize and respect these laws have resulted in the crisis humans and the planet face.

The human race is in a state of denial.

The country is just a city waiting to happen.

Expansion always leads to more expansion.

Imagine a couple living in one small room with no ability to move from this home. Now imagine that they begin adding children to that home. Regardless of the number of children they may want, it is easy to see that the absolute limit will be reached very quickly. This is our state on this planet. Regardless of the species, the earth cannot expand.

True wealth is having a healthy planet.

All species are born with intelligence; humans must attain it.

Waste is our most renewable resource.

All species struggle to survive; humans seem to struggle in vain.

Unlimited human expansion is a luxury the planet cannot afford.

Space exploration is beyond our financial means and leads people to believe the earth is disposable. What needs exploring is why we cannot live sustainably as all other creatures do.

That which gives and sustains life should be nurtured, not exterminated.

An increase in any population leads to an increase in a predatory population. Is it a surprise that microorganisms attack humans? They are our only known non-human predators.

We began managing wildlife and made it unmanageable.

It is shocking and disturbing that educated, well-informed people calmly discuss mass extinction and the destruction of the planet as if it were of little importance. It appears as just another topic on the meeting agenda.

As humans, we pride ourselves on our ability to adapt. It is also our greatest liability. Rather than solving serious problems, we simply adapt to them. This, unfortunately, is not an option for the majority of other species.

We are turning all species into scavengers. We then kill them when they do.

Even so-called natural enemies have learned to coexist on the planet. When will humans?

All species are born and die with no fanfare, recognition, or acknowledgement—no birth announcements, balloons, or gifts. After they die, they remain as insignificant to humans as when they were alive. There are no markers or monuments to memorialize one single species. Not even when the very last one marked the total extinction of a species that may have existed for millions of years. No statues to remember what that species looked like or what date they became extinct. Considering the fact that humans are largely the reason for their extinction, it is our duty to memorialize and honour their existence and acknowledge our responsibility for their devastation.

Unlike any other species, humans, even after death, continue to have a claim on land and resources, denying them to others.

We need to stop referring to the planet and its inhabitants as belonging to us. It is not "our" mountain, "our" trees, "our" oceans, "our" land, or "our" airspace. It belongs to the earth and all its inhabitants. No other species attempts to take permanent ownership of it, nor should we.

Humans spend a significant part of their lives doing nothing to help the next generation to survive. In fact, everything done puts their survival in jeopardy.

The innate responsibility to do everything to protect one's offspring, to survive, is so powerful that many species die in the process. But collectively, in humans, that seems to be an exception rather than a rule.

If we remain disconnected and lack understanding of what we need to survive, the earth will continue to be collateral damage. How many parents and children are aware that what they actually need to survive is not available at the store or via online shopping?

It was reported that a couple's infant died of starvation and neglect because both were addicted to "caring" for their virtual one. This is a condition present in one species only.

No species has to go to school, get a job to pay for food, water, or shelter to raise their young. The earth has been providing everything needed for all, including humans for eternity, and continues to do so. We have forgotten that our most critical needs are not that different from others we share the planet with.

All other species in the world, wherever they live, know how to live and raise their young. In humans, non-accidental injury is the leading cause of death for children. Why?

Regardless of circumstances or extreme conditions, all species simply just get on with living. In short "they just do it," "impossible is nothing." Ironically, these slogans humans display but rarely live up to.

In other species, only the male who has proven himself "worthy" is allowed the privilege to procreate. Even in the animal kingdom, procreating is not a "right" but a privilege that must be earned.

Sometimes males are the better parent, even in the human species.

Nature never allows species to suffer from birth to death. That is a distinctly human invention.

Ironically, humans who never required formal education have lived successfully for hundreds of thousands of years. Tribalistic societies raised healthy, self-reliant individuals who assimilated all the skills needed for survival. This provided a sense of security, and children were rarely helpless or completely dependent.

Could it be that our formal education is taking us further away from the knowledge, wisdom, and capacities required to raise strong, confident self-autonomous young people? Observations would suggest a definite *yes.*

We spend far too much time in our heads doing nothing.

The human concept of being superior to other species is not reflected in the world we have created. An insect and a flower have better survival capabilities and success than humans do since none other have mass destruction desires or capabilities.

A cancer cell continues to spread, and eventually, it too dies from killing its host. Similarly, we continue to spread our population and destruction, knowing that it cannot be sustained. We must stop.

We need to turn out the city lights so we can see the magical beauty of the stars. Nature is already providing fireworks without any form of pollution or cost.

I do not want to live in a world inhabited only by humans.

If it grows freely, we call it a weed.

The worst punishment we give to humans is to imprison them in captivity or in solitary confinement. Why do we do this to species who were free and have committed no crimes?

We create expensive, noisy and polluting machines to do what nature was already providing, free and without harm.

Only humans create that which is of no use to any other species.

The universe may be infinite, but the planet is not.

We call it sunrise and sunset because it sounds better than an earth rotation.

We have no ability to determine the actual level of intelligence of all other species. If Einstein were born unable to communicate in any form whatsoever or move his limbs, we would not have known his level of intelligence. In fact, we would likely have dismissed him as having none.

The only time a human is attacked by an animal is for legitimate reasons when protecting their young (bear) or we venture into their territory (shark). Yet, we use terms like being attacked, stalked, or other malicious connotations that are projections of human behaviour. No animal except humans' attacks without a need for self-defence.

Human encroachment on land forces animals out due to starvation, and many have become extinct. This is totally preventable.

Gifts from Mother Earth. What a generous life-giver and sustainer. Let us give her respect and gratitude by nurturing her.

There should be a law against cluttering our skyline with high rises that obstruct the view of the mountains.

I cannot imagine what it is like for a bird to return to lay eggs and care for the young, to find not only the nest gone but all the trees too. How traumatized are humans after the destruction of a hurricane?

What will we do once every square inch of the planet is covered in concrete? As water tables rise, and the land continues to disappear, nature once again reclaims itself.

I find the sound of fireworks distressing, as do many others. Imagine that sound to animals that have a high sensitivity to sound. It is traumatic and causes many to flee and get lost in their panic. Fireworks are not necessary and are harmful. They should be banned.

Humans devise systems that obstruct access to information and truth. Nature has no fear of revealing all.

RELATIONSHIPS

Look at behaviours more than you listen to words.

All human suffering is created.

A deep analysis of "suffering" often reveals the absence of sustainable principles.

I find it bizarre that people who claim to be pro-life are also pro-death penalty.

Do not approach relationships like a job. Are you getting into one because there is "nothing else" or because you are desperate?

If a relationship is not fulfilling or meeting our needs, why are we in it?

An adult who wants "unconditional love" is either still in an infantile state developmentally, or they want you to accept their conduct, however unacceptable it may be. Either way, it is very unhealthy and ill-advised.

One should never be less happy in a relationship than they were without it. If it feels wrong, get out and give yourself time to clear the clutter.

Never be in a relationship of any kind with someone you cannot trust. Never excuse lies no matter what.

Red flags are called that because they are alarms of danger that you should not ignore.

Why is it that humans have become the most powerful species on the planet but remain the most fearful?

Always be willing to accept that the person you meet and want to be with will, in fact, never change. If you want them to, then you do not want them, you want that other person you envision. Never be with someone you want to change.

In any relationship, the term "crime of passion" should be removed from our vocabulary mentality and from the legal system. This only legitimizes or minimizes violence towards another.

The term "until death do us part" is troubling. No one should have to remain in a relationship or die to leave.

Do not enter an intimate relationship with another without answering critical questions about one another. It is too late afterwards to discover your partner is not compatible as a lifelong companion, communicator, or not financially responsible. After marriage, it is too late to discover your partner is not invested in parenting and that you do not share the same values. Love will not overcome these as time goes on. In fact, it will get worse, and the marriage and children will suffer.

It is generally a mistake to "plan" a pregnancy without the agreement of the partner. It should be a joint decision rather than one person deciding or having their way. This short-term "win" often results in huge loss when the relationship rooted in deception or manipulation fractures. Doing one's "duty" leads to resentment and often "justifies" extra-marital relationships or worse.

Regardless of expectation, desire, or belief, it's best to consider that one might face being a single parent.

If a man has children from other relationships that he is not showing interest in or responsibility for, do not assume he will with you. Never have a child with anyone who does not want to be an equal parent.

Some women are addicted to being pregnant. Perhaps, too, are some men to having kids. There is no need to feed any addiction.

Many mothers are excited to have another baby but do not ensure the father is.

Many couples, particulate men, find changing diapers and crying infants an impediment to romance and attraction in the long term. Both must plan together, or they will fall apart.

Never assume that everyone wants children. In fact, it is best to assume they do not. People should start with this premise to plan their life more consciously. One should not become a parent by default.

Eyes communicate one's deepest emotions.

Sometimes things can only be understood unspoken, as air cannot be seen, only felt.

If you are not in charge or in control of your life, someone else is. This is a law of social dynamics.

Women most often questioned my decision not to have children. Their reason seemed to be "because I have to or am supposed to." These were not good reasons from my perspective. I could list off numerous reasons not to that were far more relevant and meaningful. The more reasons I gave, the more uncomfortable many became. Some became extremely hostile. Their reaction made me wonder if something deep in their subconscious was triggered. Did they have silent regrets? The ones that were totally comfortable with my choice were totally comfortable with theirs.

Someone's offer of a hand does not mean they think you weak.

I am always curious to know how couples (people) decide on how many children to have. I am shocked at how few can give a detailed, thoughtful explanation. "We just did." The single most important decision anyone can make is whether to have kids, how many, and with whom. There appears to be little discussion or planning about it. Many men seem to be "passive bystanders," often becoming fathers by default.

Some people claim they "plan to have six children" when they have not even had their first. What is this based on?

Relationships should never be about possession or ownership. Jealousy is not love.

A contract does not make a relationship; people sharing a deep connection does.

How can one person be happy in a relationship if the other is not? Yet many are in these relationships. Living in quiet desperation and resentment of a life not fully lived yet no longer "free to do so."

The vow, "Till death do us part," is being taken literally by far too many people.

People need to devise their own formula for a satisfying relationship; marriage has not been a success for many people. This is evidence of "one size does not fit all."

I would find it more disturbing to hear an affair "meant nothing" than if it did.

A successful, lifelong, loving relationship with another is more likely if it is a desire rather than a goal.

If you do not grow together, you grow apart.

It may be accurate that relationships require a lot of work, but the right one feels effortless.

Monogamy cannot be contracted or legally enforced. It must be a conscious choice and desire.

Being happy and fulfilled in a relationship for life is more like winning a lottery yet, everyone expects to achieve this.

People claim to want honesty but rarely appreciate it when they get it. Just try.

How many young men and women have lost all their dreams, hopes, and desires before they even know what they are? An unplanned pregnancy has cheated many people out of a future they will never have. Do not let this happen a second time. Take steps to be responsible while maintaining some capacity and hope to pursue your true destiny.

Men need to take a more active, assertive part in family planning and the use of contraception. It is true that a woman might make a choice to have a child without the man's agreement, consent, or involvement. However, a man cannot do so without a woman. This results in multitudes of men becoming fathers even if they did not want or plan to be. Unless there is some prior agreement, he will be required to provide financial support to the child(ren). This reality should make men take more seriously their responsibility for contraception and family planning. This is not a time to "go with the flow," as it has serious lifelong implications for all parties.

Women are at a higher risk for domestic violence and murder during pregnancy. The causes vary, but in many cases, they appear to be the result of the man deciding he does not want to be responsible for the child(ren) or the financial pressures and/or his potential lack of freedom. In other cases, where pregnancy occurred outside of a marriage, the danger that it will become public can lead to violence or the woman's death. This illustrates the importance of men taking responsibility for contraception.

In a real sense, it is a matter of life and death, usually at the cost of the pregnant woman.

Women it is ill advised to become pregnant by a married man. It leads to betrayal and deception and forces people to live double lives. The married man will not leave his wife even if the extramarital affair results in a pregnancy. She will be left a single parent. Pregnancy should never be a strategy or a means to an end.

As in nature, women need to become much more discerning about who to have a child with. Mutual attraction is not enough.

Parents are celebrated for their infinite capacity to love multiple children. I wonder why we think it impossible between adults.

Deep connections should not be vilified.

In relationships, monogamy is considered to be more a rule than it actually is. It is well documented that many men (and women) have relationships outside the marriage. It is a tragedy that people do not feel they can communicate their innermost unfulfilled needs because so often, being honest leads to total catastrophe. So, both suffer in silence.

None of us can expect our partner to remain the exact same person for the remainder of our lives. People often change with time and sometimes in dramatic ways.

Many couples have extremely happy, satisfying long-term relationships without ever getting married or living in the same household.

If two people are in a satisfying, fulfilling relationship and do not live together, there is never any doubt that they want to be with each other. Every minute they share together is a choice. People do not take the other for granted when they respect each other's need for space or self-autonomy.

Jealousy is a very destructive force. If someone you desire chooses to be with another, set them free. You cannot and should not try and own or possess any living being.

Do not treat others how you want to be treated; that is projection. Treat others how they want to be treated.

Actively seek out mentors who are living a life of meaning and purpose, and never lose your connection to them.

Invest in relationships, not perceived security.

There are many who chose to have children, so they have someone care for them in their elder years, only to find they are utterly alone.

Healthy resolution of disagreements improves self-development and relationships.

People who avoid disagreement or conflicts out of fear take you further away from your truth. It is like taking endless detours away from your destination.

Authentic generosity is a reflection of spirituality.

In matriarchal societies, women were worshipped for their role as life-givers. These societies tended to be peaceful. All males cared for the children since none was certain which children they fathered. There was no sense of ownership or rejection of children. Raising them was a shared responsibility.

Tribal societies generally raised healthy, confident, self-autonomous children. By age twelve, they could survive fairly independently. The best one can provide to their child is to make them resilient and independent as quickly as possible. So-called modern societies are doing the opposite. Children are dependent upon adults for longer periods of time.

It would serve people better if it were more difficult to get married but easier to get divorced. It would allow for more thought and possibly prevent expensive legal consequences and, in many cases, hostility or even violence.

There is no greater loneliness than being in a loveless, meaningless relationship.

After a breakup, you may feel lonely, but take enough time, and you will discover this will be replaced with a sense of freedom. Do not rush into being in a relationship. Learn first how to be with yourself without fear and anxiety.

If you hurt someone, do not make it about yourself and quickly heal it. No one needs to suffer.

A true measure of your self-worth is how you feel about yourself when doing nothing.

Be with yourself without distraction.

If your self-worth is rooted in something external, you are in danger of losing it. If it is rooted in who you are, you are not.

Religions divide, spirituality unites.

Why do religions glorify heaven as a place of ultimate glory and nirvana but are so fearful of death? They are against suicide and assisted death. This contradiction is never explained.

Kids are expected to attend school for twelve years and be qualified for absolutely nothing. Not a proposition any adult would accept. No one admits the primary purpose of the education system is a place for children to go while their parents are at work. Having kids in school for eight hours a day from kindergarten on is counterproductive to learning, and for many, also counterproductive for psychological and physical development and well-being.

How can we teach children to respect life when we continue to destroy it?

People need to allow more honesty within their relationships, so people do not feel compelled to lie.

Violence perpetuates more violence. Just as children are affected by witnessing domestic violence, they may become future victims or perpetrators because their parents modelled this behaviour. It does not need to be taught or even spoken about, but the message about what is acceptable or not is ingrained in their psyche. This is how we raise generations to treat each other, animals, and the planet.

Contrary to what many think about relationships, one plus one does not equal everything.

Guns do not kill people; people do. Then do not give people guns.

We have created a world that requires humans to have psychological and unhealthy behaviours to live. A certain amount of pathology seems to have become the "norm." How else can billions of us live with the world we have created, but for dissociation, lack of empathy, denial, duplicity, and narcissism?

What comes first, a psychological disorder, then the behaviour, or is it the reverse?

Despite societies where government programs have "assumed" the role of providers or helpers, the incidence of dysfunctions, fears, and phobias continues to increase. Consider the paradox. That is not to suggest people do not require support. It is because we have eliminated natural support systems by promoting complete individualism that ultimately does not help the individual or community. Government response will always be inadequate and unsustainable.

It is ironic that the greater the population, the greater the emphasis is on individuality. The areas that have smaller populations have a greater emphasis on the collective community. A model for "community" artificially designed by humans results in the exact opposite. In less populated areas, people have a need and desire to come together. In dense cities, people want to get "space" from each other.

In a tribal society that relies on obtaining food by climbing tall trees, it is unlikely the tribe will develop a fear of heights. In a tribe where consuming insects is necessary for survival; it would be impossible for any of them to develop a fear of insects.

MEDIA

The news is not.

Just say no, to consumerism

The one with the most toys loses.

Nothing is more threatening to the corporate world than having fewer humans on the planet.

The news paralyzes people through fear, which prevents them from uniting and creating change.

"Advertising"—a tool used to confuse our priorities.

The "news" does not inform or educate us. It serves as a distraction from the truth about what is actually happening in the world. It is served up with the same menu every single day. How does it help me or the world to learn there was a car accident? The main effect of the "news" promotes fear and a sense of hopelessness. Is this a coincidence, or does it serve the real purpose? The more apathetic and powerless we feel, the less likely we will focus on issues that demand our attention and that we need to fight for.

How many species, vital to our survival and that of the planet, have been affected or annihilated? How many of them were raising their young in those trees? How many bees that were helping humans and the planet to survive were massacred? Where are the daily "breaking news headlines" about this most important information? This is not accidental. It is by design.

We should be regularly told how many humans any geography can support in relation to available resources (predictions of employment numbers, available hospital beds, standard of living). Just like every other species is required to maintain a balance, so should we. We are never told, nor is that even a consideration. We are locked into a prison that is based on increasing the number of humans, increasing consumption, and increasing the destruction of the planet. Repeat, repeat, repeat.

The worst tool we could have introduced to young people, especially teens, is a so-called "smart" device. Taking selfies, "looking," good, being the most "liked" and popular has become an accepted substitute for actual accomplishments and real success for far too many. The adults have readily allowed this.

If the image of someone is used for commercial display or marketing purposes, that person is financially compensated. It is time that humans begin donating money to the cause when an image of an animal or nature is used. Their images are used in sports teams, sports uniforms, or mascots by major corporations. They should be paying compensation for the protection and survival of the species they use in their marketing. These images are not displayed to honour the species but to reduce cost by not using the "valuable" costly image of a human. Corporations using images of an animal should provide monetary compensation to a Trust that is put towards the protection of the animal.

If our marketing skills could be utilized to save the planet, we could have achieved it by now.

People will line up outside, regardless of temperature or time, sometimes for days, to buy the newest designer item, regardless of cost but become outraged if there is a slight increase or tax to pay to make the planet cleaner and safer.

It is absurd that in movies and the news, we cast other species on the planet as potential killers to be feared and killed, though nothing is further from the truth.

Human's love making movies about unlikely forces such as aliens, dark forces, or asteroids, creating an unrealistic perceived threat to the survival of humans. This is a diversion to keep us from focusing on the more immediate threat to the planet, which is us.

Movies about human overpopulation and overconsumption are glaringly absent.

It is curious that our economy is set up for an ever-increasing population that is unsustainable. People with children are given tax breaks despite using the highest amount of services and infrastructure, while people with no kids pay the highest. If people are given financial incentives, having smaller families will be less likely. This needs to be reversed.

People should pay for the amount of resources they use. If a family of six uses less than a couple, the family of six should pay less.

PARTING THOUGHTS

Nothing we do is "out there," whether it is dumping waste, pollution, or poisons. It is all right here beside us in our very homes and the earth. Time to declare peace. Time to start using our so-called intelligence to find solutions for living peacefully, fairly, and justly. This must be done on a global level. We have plenty of money that we will save from having a "no-war" policy, and that will begin to provide for necessities, and collectively, we need to heal from what we have been doing to each other. We need to acknowledge and grieve for the violence we have inflicted on the planet and on all the beautiful creatures, plants, and flowers that bring life and beauty to the planet and to our lives. We do not need the idle worship of abstract gods or human images of God. We need to worship life on the planet, the earth. Without the earth, we will not exist. We must turn our focus and attention to building back what we have destroyed. They all just need to spot to live, eat, and raise their young as we do. They are not at war with us. They peacefully go about life. We rarely see or even hear them. Live and let live.

We should be much more concerned about protecting what we absolutely need to stay alive. Air is something we can only go without for a few seconds. Think about that. Without that in our lungs, we die, or our brain literally dies from lack of oxygen. This is our number one priority. We need viable soil for plants and trees. They are our lungs, and we must preserve them. All the insects required to pollinate need to be protected. Bees have been doing this, and all the while, we take and profit from tons of their delicious honey and exterminate them. We need to find and show our gratitude to earth and all our fellow community members. So, let's let them live. That is all we are required to do. It isn't much. We can, and we must do it. This is the right thing for the planet and for us. People with children who have concerns for their future can only preserve the planet if they start turning their attention to the life-giving properties and creatures on the planet. There is no other way. Personally, I enjoy walking through trails, smelling flowers, and listening to the sounds or creatures going about their day. They are truly living in the moment, sitting on a leaf or branch or rolling around in the mud, playing with other animals. They are living in the paradise we also live in. But we must stop destroying it. It need not be hell. It can remain paradise. We can do it. We are, after all, intelligent, creative, inventive, and adaptable. We just need to improve our mindset, get rid of our silly notions of being entitled and superior to all other species. We just need to nurture the paradise, and it will continue giving as there can again be plenty. We just must remember that we need to share. Not hoard and be greedy to the detriment to others, humans or not.

Let's marvel in the wonder, beauty, and abundance of life nature has created for us to share with all in it. It truly is a sacred place to respect and give back to.

The planet is a paradise. Its beauty is stunning. Every flower, the stars, the moon, sunrises, mountains, the oceans, every creature is a miracle of nature. I want to see the animals and plants that reside in all those places, in their natural habitat—just living, raising their young and bringing beauty by just being. Listen to the hoots and howls and chirps—the soothing sounds of waves. Where nature is, there is peace and balance. Where humans are, there is devastation and war and a planet under the worst neglect and abuse in its history. You can't find "ugly" in nature. It does not exist. Let's no longer ignore the collective screams and wails of all the species, crying for our help. If they no longer have to fear us, they can regain their important role in the ecosystem, and we need them to. Let nature reclaim more of herself, so once again, the air, water and all ecosystems can become as pristine as they were for billions of years. Nature is not giving up and will rebound quickly.

We have seen it during Covid. Once we can live in peace with each other and on the planet, we can again venture out to see the planet, as will all the creatures. We can follow nature once again and use the blueprint for survival—what a relief. We no longer need to be responsible. We never really were. We just deluded ourselves for a while. Now that we know the truth, the comforting truth, it is in far more capable hands. Billions of years of success can't be wrong. Nature knows how to do Life.

How nature does with nonhumans following its blueprint for living in all its biodiversity, beauty and abundance.

ODE TO SOCIAL WORK

From the start, I quickly knew
This work could only be done by few
Because one has to give more than one can give
To allow others a chance to live
For this, one needs a tough mind that is smart
But along with this, soft must be the heart
To find this balance is difficult indeed
For most, it is challenging to meet others' needs
To view the world, through the eyes of a child
Is not something one can learn in school or in the wild
Even children that we may not know
has the right to be loved, be nourished to grow
And when that child looks to us for protection
For not a split second does this require reflection
Little souls, already beaten and forsaken
They are our utmost priority; never be mistaken
Each one special and unique in every way
But very much the same in what they need every day
To live in a world in which they are the centre
Protected, supported and provided with mentors
Help steer the child away from their fears
To see them smile, instead of filled with tears

To work hard and shield them from pain
Is the only thing that keeps many of us sane
The children we work for are able to feel,
Which of us care and help them to heal
They are incredibly insightful and astute
Filled with charm, character, and real cute
They need caring adults to help show the way
But first, we need to prove we are worthy of having a say
If one remains fiercely committed to their cause
They will learn to trust without giving pause
Because no matter what may be their history
What they need now is never a mystery
Ideally they need a village to care
Or maybe even just one, if one so dares
"Never give up on me," they say,
is what keeps me coming back, day after day
There is no other work like this
One small mistake and a life can be missed
For these children, every second counts
A mistake is something that comes back to haunt
That children's existence needs celebration
That they expect the most from us is not a revelation
Pushing any system always comes with a cost
A lonely voice in the dark, and lost
But unless you have a fiercely dedicated team
Doing one's best for children will
tragically remain a dream

With gratitude,
Arwinder Kaur
2012

REFERENCES

The main cause of deforestation is agriculture (but poorly planned infrastructure is emerging as a big threat too), and the main cause of forest degradation is illegal logging. In 2019, the tropics lost close to thirty soccer fields' worth of trees every single minute. https://www.worldwildlife.org/threats/deforestation-and-forest-degradation

About 385,000 babies are born each day, according to the UN. That adds up to more than 140 million a year. The 140 million extra babies per year join a world population projected to reach 10 billion people by 2056.

https://www.theworldcounts.com/stories/how-many-babies-are-born-each-day

Just in the US, reusable cloth baby diapers stop an estimated half-ton of disposable diapers per child from going into US landfills each year and cut down on pathogens that could leak into the water supply.

https://www.prnewswire.com/news-releases/disposable-diapers-add-millions-of-tons-of-waste-to-landfills-each-year-according-to-epa-report-300384344.html

In Canada, the parliament is responsible for approving budgets, and this does not involve the taxpayers. I am proposing that rather than put the onus on every taxpayer to try and make sense of the numerous volumes of information and how money is allocated and spent, I believe it is the duty of the peoples' government to proactively provide this to every taxpayer. I wish to receive a monthly statement from each level of government by email so I can review the budget and how it is being spent in real-time, not be told once a year or after an audit. By then, it is too late. Also, I want information by email on surplus and discretionary spending in order to have input into how it is allocated. It is not appropriate to keep every taxpayer in the dark about our money, and the onus should not be on us. Most people find bureaucracy and trying to make sense of it very arduous. It is our money, and we need a user-friendly way of getting the information and giving input. If there is misspending or corruption, it needs to be reported directly to the taxpayer, so we know which party was responsible and how the money is going to be put back into the peoples' fund. We do not need to be told years later that these things happen. This is the only way to make government officials accountable and transparent by monthly reporting to the people.

https://lop.parl.ca/sites/PublicWebsite/default/en_CA/ResearchPublications/201541E

RELEVANT BOOKS ON WHICH I BASE MY INFORMATION

All writings of Daniel Quinn: *Ishmael, My Ishmael, Beyond Civilization, Providence,* and *The Story of B. There are numerous websites related to Quinn his work and followers.*

Four Arguments for the Elimination of Television by Jerry Mander

The Unschooling Unmanual by Jan Hunt

Our Angry Earth by Asimov, Isaac, Pohl, and Frederik

Toxics and Health: The Potential Long-Term Effects of Industrial Activity by Cheryl Simon Silver

There are many environmental organizations with resources like everyday products that are safe for the planet such as The David Suzuki Foundation. Search for your own.

There is many organizations working to improve treatment of animals such as:

The Nonhuman Project, Adopt a Chimp, numerous organizations to support conservation and protection of the planet.

Please search for organizations that have to do with supporting people protecting the Amazon Forest, Conservation, protection of all species and planet.

In lieu of buying products for gifts donate to important organizations that need our support..

A movement to create cruelty free meat is happening such as Paul Shapiro author of *Clean Meat: How Growing Meat without Animals will Revolutionize Dinner and the World.*

Many podcasts and free streaming sites allow access to vast amount of information not being covered on mainstream media. WaterBear is an app that has a collection of short films to show all the positive work being done and progress being made around the planet. It is important to tap into these to remind us there is hope and many groups are coming together to do the right thing. People with a compass.

Please note that some links may become outdated. All the information I refer to is readily available through internet searches.

CPSIA information can be obtained
at www.ICGtesting.com
Printed in the USA
BVHW092058311021
620415BV00014BA/214